More praise ~~for Holiday ~~

Sibyl is a wonderful Christmas historian and unique New Yorker—intelligent, caring and so very interesting. Her experience guiding tour groups for NBC and NYCVP for years gave her access to the people and places that make New York so special over the Christmas holidays. If anyone knows Christmas in New York—it is Sibyl McCormac Groff—the "spirited" New Yorker!

—**Barry Tenenbaum,** President, New York City
Vacations, Inc.

Sibyl Groff—"The Spirited New Yorker"—has done it again! From her very personal perspective, your very own Christmas Elf will guide you through the Christmas holidays in New York City. From a specialist in New York Christmas touring programs, you'll learn of the histories of Christmas traditions, notable sights you should definitely see, unusual holiday activities, and the joys to be shared by a lover of a New York Christmas! Curl up with a cup of hot chocolate, stir it with a peppermint candy cane, and dream of joyous and exciting holiday activities. Carry this playful (and useful) guidebook with you as you discover the magic of the Christmas holidays!

—**Justin Ferate,** Noted Urban Historian: Selected by the Governor of New York and the New York State Tourism Council as "New York's Most Engaging Tour Guide"

DEAR EMMA,
HOW GRATIFYING TO
MEET YOU — EMMA- my
MOTHER'S NAME. I FEEL SHE
IS THRILLED THAT SUCH A

New York Christmas

Ho-ho-ho at Gothamtide!™

by Sibyl McCormac Groff

BRIGHT, LOVELY AND
FUN YOUNG LADY HAS HER
NAME!
CONTINUE TO SPRINKLE
JOY!!! Sibyl   HO!
                    HO!
                    HO!

"7th" AUGUST 2019

ISBN 13: 978-1539506126

For all inquiries please contact Sibyl McCormac Groff at: spirsib@gmail.com

Text set in Chaparral Pro
Designed by Sarah McElwain
First Edition

Printed in the United States of America

DEDICATION

Hohoho! became affiliated with Christmas when New Yorker Clement Clarke Moore wrote "A Visit from St. Nicholas" who "laughed like a bowl full of jelly"in the 1820s. Later the illustrations by cartoonist - illustrator Thomas Nast, beginning in the 1860s, made Santa the jolly robust man, who said "hohoho! "

Hohoho is known as a happy greeting and sound. It has acquired many meanings through the years. A study was just done in Hungary titled, "Where the ho ho hos are," denoting where the happiest people in the country live.

Hohoho was also the shepherds' call to their sheep. Heartfelt thanks to my special "shepherds" Jeannie Bochette, Sandi D'Andrea, Elizabeth Leckie, John Martine, Jonathan "Princess" Preece and William Spink, together with my editor, Sarah McElwain, who have given their time, advice, expertise, encouragement and hohohos!

To the glittering "stars" in the sky
who have shared my love for Gothamtide
and whose "light"
is still radiant and inspiring.

MARGARET D. MCCORMAC

BILLIE BRITZ

GWEN KOCH

Contents

I
INTRODUCTION

Ho-ho-ho! Greetings from Sibyl, a New Yorker, who loves Christmas in New York City —The Christmas Capital! I have loved Christmas ever since I was a wee one and years ago stayed at The Plaza, the elegant hotel on Fifth Avenue by Central Park, the center of Christmas cheer. I was inspired when I saw all the horse drawn carriages and by my capricious friend, Eloise. In case you don't know her, she is the devilish little girl who lived in The Plaza and caused havoc all the time but is fun, fun, and fun! In fact when the book "Eloise: A Book for Precocious Grown-ups" by Kay Thompson was published in 1955, I received several copies from friends who thought that I was a grown-up version of this mirthful 6-year-old. The illustrations by Hilary Knight are enchanting and Eloise's spirit still inspires many of us. She motivated me to research and write a Christmas letter about all the beautiful, illuminating festivities and decorations in New York. For about thirty-five years I have sent this gleeful "Gothamtide" (a word I have coined and will explain later in the booklet) greetings to friends around the world. I have studied in depth many aspects of this favorite and inspiring holiday and have written about Christmas for several prestigious publications including *The Magazine* ANTIQUES and *Flower Magazine*. As The Spirited New Yorker, I give lectures and tours, as well as television interviews.

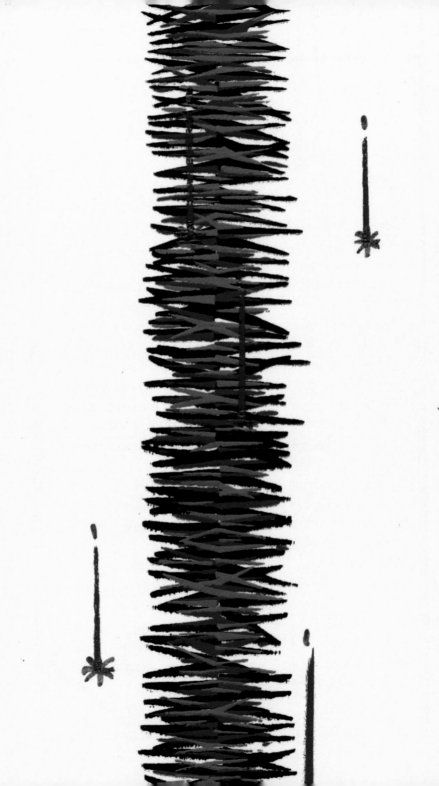

Over the years I have acquired many other nicknames, including: Queen Santa, the Elf, Lady Gothamtide and The Lady in Red.

This booklet contains my recommendations and remembrances of so many happenings and festivities. It's a guide to the spectacular New York City spirit at Christmas. As a dedicated Rockefeller Center historian and tour guide since 2001, a lot of these Gothamtide recollections are sparked by my experiences in this magical Christmas mosaic all year. Queen Santa of The Tree could write a lot more but I've decided that I am tired of carrying heavy books around and want to share my tidbits in a wee portable booklet.

My brother Dean added that he had a paper route when he was about 11 and I was 8. As one of our Christmas capers we also brought along hot dish mats to sell that we had woven. I remember carrying a box that said "The McCormac Mat Company"' with samples. The proceeds went towards gifts for our menagerie and others!

To return to the awakening of my Christmas spirit, I grew up in upstate New York in a family that loved Christmas. My brother and I had lots of stuffed animals including bears, pandas, and monkeys brought back to us by our father from his travels. When I was about six, I felt that our animal buddies should have their own Christmas tree in a separate room. My parents agreed. I decorated this little tree and also learned how to knit sweaters and hats to give to our stuffed animals. Bill Panda still has his Christmas sweater.

By the time I was ten, there was a sign on my bedroom door: "Santa's North Pole." One year my godfather dared to open the door and found me sitting on the floor wrapping presents to give away to classmates, neighbors and relatives. Later I started making Christmas ornaments out of felt and embroidered with candy canes, trees and Santa Clauses to give to friends. Many of these still adorn my friends' Christmas trees. *So come and jingle along with me!*

HOW TO USE THIS BOOK & GUIDELINES

There are so many aspects of Christmas that can be experienced in New York City: Look at the glittering lights on the many trees, stores, windows, and statues; see Santa Claus; listen and/or sing along to all sorts of holiday music ranging from sacred to carols; learn about the history of Christmas traditions by visiting historic houses and museums; stroll around and enjoy a wide variety of holiday food and ambiance.

Times are changing. "Glitz, glamour, gems and glitter" are proving to be the most fashionable. Santa, crèches, elves and traditional holiday displays are not as prevalent as each year things change. Please note that I am only concentrating on Manhattan, especially Rockefeller Center and Midtown, as there is so much to see and do. Queen Santa has so much Gothamtide knowledge and the other four boroughs of New York City have their Christmas treats, but my goal is to make this a small remembrance treasure.

Gothamtide traditions are important as well as the vitality and energy that permeates everyone —New Yorkers and tourists—during the holiday season. I just love walking the streets and taking in the scene! An added dimension is the snow, which brings its own magic and patterns. "Let it snow, let it snow." But hopefully, not like the blizzard I got caught in several years ago on Christmas Day when I was giving a tour. My Rockefeller Center tree was shaking and bending. As the winds accelerated, the snow blinded the people on my tour. Thank heavens we were at the end of the tour by The Tree. How fortunate I was when I headed home that a cab driver actually saw my red coat and drove me to my front door! The wind was so fierce that when I got into my building it took me about fifteen minutes before I realized that my red hat was missing.

I dashed outside and hidden in a pile of snow forming so quickly, I pulled out my hat! *(Yes, Virginia There is a Santa Claus or is it the magic of Gothamtide again!)*

By the way, wear something red—red is a happy color. The dictionary says, "Red's meaning includes energy, power, strength, desire and love." I have a red coat and hat and often carry a candy cane. Many people stop me and say, "Thanks for brightening my day and New York Christmas." Sometimes I wear my big green badge that reads, "The fat man is coming."

This "Lady in Red" strikes up spontaneous conversations as I stroll about with a smile on my face. As I meander, I sometimes give out little candy canes to other merrymakers. Their joyful smiles and thanks are the season's gift to me. Some comments include: "You and your hat are radiant!"

Remember to look up at the buildings. All the decorative "beasties" and other architectural decorations bring joy. Try to find some. Many buildings have these applied decorations made of plaster or other materials around their entrances, on the facades or toward the top. You might see rosettes, figures, leaves, angels, flowers and birds. There are often animals, the most popular being lions. If you want to see "rats" go to the side entrance of Grand Central Terminal on

Lexington and 43rd Street. At the adjacent Graybar Building you will see them scurrying up the lines holding up the canopy! This is not very Christmas-y but Grand Central is.

Don't be bashful. Most New Yorkers and tourists are very friendly and helpful! There are so many festive things to see and do. Venues, events and decorations are constantly changing. Here are a few suggestions: Look at NYCVP.com, a full service travel agency that I have happily been involved with for years, which has many tours (look out for Queen Santa), tickets and informative suggestions. Check out the *New York Times, Time Out, Wall Street Journal*, and the free *Metro* paper, Carnegie Hall and Lincoln Center listings. Think about getting The New York Pass®, which gives discounts for many festive Gothamtide events at The Metropolitan Museum of Art, The American Museum of Natural History, The Empire State Building, the Top of the Rock and Circle Line Boat Tours. Also, check out New York City's official tourist bureau at: nycgo.com. There are many useful apps and websites. Please note that eateries are mentioned only if I have dined happily!

If you have time do take a boat tour to see the dazzling lights, combined with carol singing and cocoa sipping—or something stronger! And take a bus tour or drive around the periphery of the city, circling from FDR Drive to the West Side Highway to see radiant and exhilarating Gotham. If I included all that I wanted this would be a huge volume. So only the most important buildings and things get a lot of detail.

Be inspired by
Ralph Waldo Emerson
who wrote, "sprinkle joy!"

II
GOTHAMTIDE™

*B*efore we jingle, let me explain how I coined the word Gothamtide! Christmas is traditionally the happiest, most sacred, festive and beautiful holiday of the year. To me, New York City is the Christmas capital of the U.S. because it was the original site of so many Christmas happenings, which led to its becoming the most important holiday of the year by the end of the 19th century.

I also realize that the word "Christmas" does not reflect the many aspects of this holiday both here and around the world. Furthermore, in today's world, the word "Christmas" turns some scrooges off! I therefore have created the word "Gothamtide" to reflect the commonalities of the diverse secular, vernacular and universal aspects of holidays from different countries and religions. I chose the word for its many New York connections.

"Gotham" is an actual small town (with a population of about 1,500) seven miles south of Nottingham, England. In a popular legend originating in medieval times the residents began acting strangely when King John (1199–1216) wanted to build a road through "goat town," which later became Gotham. The villagers jumped around, acting mad and doing strange things like erecting a fence around a bush so a cuckoo would not escape. In those days bizarre behavior was feared as a contagious disease so the road was not built. I met people from Gotham once on a Rockefeller Center tour and we literally did jump with glee when they found out that I knew about their "goat town."

Washington Irving, one of the first distinguished American authors who combined fun, fact and fancy, coined the word "Gotham" in "Chronicles of The Renowned and Ancient City of Gotham," published in the literary magazine *Salmagundi* in 1809 to show that New Yorkers were buffoons too. (And some of us still are! Ha and ho!) The name caught on right away. In case you are wondering, the Gotham that appeared in Batman in 1939 was copied from Irving! The word "tide" is an Old English word for "celebration," and defined as a "definite time, place of season in a day, year, life" in *The New Shorter Oxford English Dictionary*, 1993.

On Christmas Day George Washington crossing the Delaware en route to Trenton with his troops supposedly said, "Christmas restores the spirits of men"!

But let's go back to pre-Christian times. The importance of greenery, trees, lights, feasting and gifts has its origins in pagan and ancient cultures, which observed such holidays as the Winter Solstice, marking the shortest day and longest night of the year, and Saturnalia, a Roman festival honoring the deity Saturn. With the acceptance of Christianity in the 4th century, these earlier traditions were reinterpreted and continue to be.

As the world becomes increasingly global, it is fascinating to learn about other cultures and their holidays. I love talking to strangers and cab drivers about Gothamtide. A Sikh cab driver told me that he has a niche in his home with religious statues, a candle and Santa Claus. Someone from Thailand told me how at their holy days candles are floated in the water in lotus cups called "Loy Krathong." In India, Diwali is celebrated with rows of lights. "Carols by Candlelight" is an Australian tradition. In

Japan and Hong Kong many homes have decorated Christmas trees. A recent article in the *Wall Street Journal* (July 8, 2016, page A11) by Sabeeha Rehman, author of "Threading My Prayer Rug: One Woman's Journey from Pakistani Muslim to American Muslim," tells the story of how she and her friends made Eid, the end of Ramadan in  July, more of a holiday with lights, feasting and gifts because of the importance of Christmas in American life. But her son was still upset on Christmas Day because there was no tree. She never got him one. He is now grown up and married and has a small tree in his home. New York City is bursting with international tourists and residents and I always try to talk to them about the commonalities among these holiday celebrations.

Some Texans I met told me that in the part of their state settled by Germans, it is a tradition to hide a glass pickle in the Christmas tree. Whoever finds the pickle gets an additional gift and good luck for the year. This custom started in Lauscha, Germany, where glass ornaments were first blown in the 1870s. I look forward to hearing about your Christmas customs too!

Let's be jolly with some holly!

III
A HISTORY
OF CHRISTMAS IN
NEW YORK CITY

Since I started feeling the New York Christmas spirit over thirty years ago, I have researched and continued to learn about the Christmas capital. New Yorkers have long promoted the Christmas season or "Gothamtide," which begins in early December and lasts for twelve days or until Twelfth Night. Did you know that Christmas was not a legal holiday until 1870 when Congress finally passed the legislation? If you are from Alabama, be proud that your state was the first to make Christmas a legal holiday in 1836. New York did not until 1849.

New York's prosperous ports (enhanced by the opening of the Erie Canal in 1825), the development of the transcontinental railroad system, and the rise of industry and commerce led to an increase in the number of immigrants settling in the city and the emergence of the family-centered middle class. New York City was the biggest producer of early print publications, which spread Christmas to everyone around the country.

This melting pot and port city is fortunate that settlers brought their holiday traditions from different countries. Among them, the Germans who gave us the Christmas tree, gift-giving and "stollen" (a Christmas pastry); the Dutch with Saint Nicholas and his buddy, "Black Peter," the stocking, and cookies; the French contributed caroling, and the nummy "Buche de noel;" the English feasting, the Boar's head, Christmas card, mumming, pantomimes and Christmas pudding; the Italians created Befana, the old woman who brings gifts, the Nativity and hand-crafted figures from Naples; the Japanese the origami tree and the Swedish St. Lucy's Day.

Can you believe that as New York City grew so did the pre-Christian Saturnalia holiday rituals including rowdiness, drunkenness and shooting of firecrackers? (Please don't follow these customs!) Lydia Maria Child wrote in 1843, "I never heard such a firing in of the new." The poor woman retreated to her bed and was kept awake all night. By the end of the nineteenth century, however, such excesses of the season waned with the emergence of the celebration of Christmas as a familial day. In 1884, Charles Dudley Warner, a noted author observed, "We had saved out of the past nearly all that was good...the revived Christmas of our time is no doubt better than the old."

Four New Yorkers were particularly responsible for the growing acceptance of the familial Christmas led by a spirited Santa Claus. Washington Irving, John Pintard, Clement Clarke Moore and Thomas Nast reconstituted these traditions including turning saintly Saint Nicholas into secular Santa Claus in popular publications. The tradition of giving presents to children evolved from the Dutch celebration of the feast day of Saint Nicholas on December 6th. Saint Nicholas, a 4th century bishop from Myra (Turkey today) was known for his good deeds to children, mariners and the less fortunate. Do you know that this saint performed many miracles, including bringing three children back to life? Think of all the churches named for him all over the world. In 1810 John Pintard, (a founder of the New-York Historical Society in 1804) created a flyer for the first St. Nicholas Day Celebration. This poem-song "Santa Claus, Good Holy Man" showed saintly St. Nicholas giving gifts to children.

In 1809, as mentioned above, Washington Irving wrote "Knickerbocker's History of New York." In this early major contribution to American comic literature, Irving satirizes the customs, culture, and political climate of New York during the early nineteenth century. Irving created the moniker, "Diedrich Knickerbocker," which became the name for old Dutch and Gotham families. He introduced the Dutch "Sinterklaas" having a jolly ride in the air in a horse drawn wagon, smoking a pipe, and bringing gifts down the chimney on December 6. Irving created the legendary figure of St. Nicholas on the bow of an early Dutch ship sailing to America and made him the Patron Saint of New York. Saint Nicholas was becoming our secular Santa Claus.

His friend, Clement Clarke Moore, wrote "A Visit from St. Nicholas" or "The Night Before Christmas" in 1822 for his children. St. Nicholas becomes a jolly old elf with no religious affiliation. This poem was published in the *Troy Sentinel* newspaper the following year. In those days newsboys delivered the papers. These news carriers recited or gave out this poem at Christmas for tips. It was quickly picked up and published by other newspapers. It is interesting that Moore did not take credit for the transformation of the St. Nicholas story until 1837, when he called it "a trifle." In the first illustrations in 1844 this elf-like figure was a besotted person who did not look like St. Nicholas. The plot thickened when the Livingston family claimed that their patriarch, Henry Livingston wrote the poem. This Hudson River patroon was a contemporary of Moore's and known for his humorous writing. The family lost this evidence

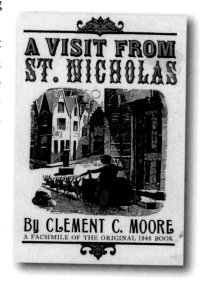

A VISIT FROM ST. NICHOLAS

BY CLEMENT C. MOORE
A FACSIMILE OF THE ORIGINAL 1848 BOOK

OLD
CHRISTMAS.

FROM & THE
Sketch of Book
Washington Irving.

ILLUSTRATED BY
R. CALDECOTT

London.
Macmillan & Co

1876

but their belief was substantiated by a professor who studied both Moore's and Livingston's writings and found the writing to definitely be Livingston's.

Santa Claus, as we know him today, evolved from the illustrations of political cartoonist, Thomas Nast, who loved this Christmas icon and created illustrations for *Harper's Weekly* between 1863 and 1886. Nast, who created this robust, jolly, gift-giving character invented Santa's "workshop" in the North Pole, Santa looking through his telescope "for good children" and Santa's account book with a "record of behavior." (Do get the reprint of his book "Thomas Nast's Christmas Drawings of 1890.")

In 1819–1820 Washington Irving wrote another highly successful volume, "The Sketch Book of Geoffrey Crayon, Gent." Romantically describing an old-fashioned Christmas in an apocryphal English country house called Bracebridge Hall, Irving waxed on about the family coming home to celebrate Christmas by attending church, feasting, playing games, dancing and spreading goodwill to the community.

Magazines and printed publications featured articles on all aspects of Christmas, such as how to make wreaths, "cornucopia" tree ornaments, handmade knitted and crocheted gifts, holiday food, and games. The tradition of the Christmas tree originated in Germany before being brought to England and the United States. The New York diarist, Charles Haswell recalled, "I have a vivid remembrance of going over to Brooklyn (in the 1830s) to witness...the novelty of German families dressing a Christmas tree."

A popular illustration of Queen Victoria, Prince Albert and their family in front of a Christmas tree on a table adorned with candles, tinsel, glass and paper ornaments promoted Christmas. First published in the December 1848 issue of the "Illustrated London News" it was featured in the American magazine, "Godey's Lady's Book" in 1850. The Royal Couple and family were so admired in America at the time that the illustration increased the importance of family holiday celebrations and Christmas trees. The invention of a tree stand by Albrecht and Mott of Philadelphia in 1876 heightened the allure of Christmas trees. F. W. Woolworth's "5 and 10 cent" stores capitalized on selling glass, and metal ornaments imported from Germany. Soon the home became the center of merry-making with carols, games, dancing and feasting. Until the latter part of the 19th century most gifts were given on New Year's Day or Twelfth Night on January 6th. Many went to Barnum's Circus, the opera or a dance on Christmas Day. The development of Sunday schools, shopping and department stores furthered the acceptance and celebration of Christmas. By the 1880s "The Golden Age of the Old Fashioned Tree" was created and is still golden!

> "Over the winter glaciers I see the summer glow, and through the wide-piled snowdrift the warm rosebuds below."
>
> —Ralph Waldo Emerson

Another New Yorker, Edward H. Johnson, who worked with Thomas Edison at the Edison Illuminating Company, strung light bulbs together and created a twinkling tree in 1882. In 1903 General Electric started selling strands of lights. Many different types of lighting have since been developed like today's LEDs.

As we have noted, the printed word has always spread so many aspects of Christmas. Think of the importance of the letter to Francis P. Church, editor of *The New York Sun*, from an 8-year old girl, Virginia O'Hanlon who wanted to know if there was a Santa Claus. On September 21, 1897 he replied with a creative support for the existence of Santa Claus stating, "Nobody sees Santa Claus, but that is no sign that there is no Santa Claus. The most real things in the world are those that neither children nor men can see." His answer, "Yes, Virginia, there is a Santa Claus," is still depicted at Macy's. Go see Virginia at the department store where her spirit is present each year. Her motto and the store's is "I Believe." And so does Eloise! Maybe this will inspire you to write something too.

Santa Claus officially married in 1889, with publication of "Goody Santa Claus on a Sleigh Ride" by Katharine Lee Bates, which was featured in *The New York World* the same year.

Goody means "good wife," which Mrs. Santa has been called ever since. Since then many other customs have been created, which I will tell you about in another Yuletime.

CHARITY & GIVING

*T*o me charity or giving is so important and is particularly prevalent during the Christmas season. Charity fairs in the 19th century promoted giving to the less fortunate. On December 26, 1882, *The New York Tribune* wrote, "Nowhere in Christendom are the poor remembered at Christmastide so generously." This has blossomed and every holiday it is rewarding to know that so many stores offer merchandise with a percentage going to non-profits. Several years ago Lady Gaga had many products at Barneys made especially for Christmas. Twenty-five percent of the profits went to her anti-bullying campaign. I still have some of her tasteful tea.

Like Lady Gaga, Prince or the Beatles, the English author Charles Dickens, who wrote the book, "A Christmas Carol" in 1843 was a "rock star." When he lectured in New York in 1867, Dickens was so popular that tickets were scalped and admirers fainted when they saw him talk about his "carol" philosophy of humanitarianism, which included the family and charity. Incidentally, when he died several years later some thought that Christmas would die too! Oh what lovely thoughts he left: "Many merry Christmases, friendships, cheerful recollections, affection on earth, and heaven at last for all of us. And to quote Tiny Tim: "God bless us, every one!"

Dickens influenced many social reformers like Jacob Riis, a Danish immigrant and journalist, who captured with his writing and camera the dreadful living conditions of the poor in New York City. Riis' renowned book, "How the Other Half Lives" was published in 1889. Teddy Roosevelt, the New York City Police Commissioner, was so impressed at the time that he sought out Riis and the two walked the streets observing the sad scenes. Roosevelt and Riis promoted social welfare legislation, such as closing existing lodging

Giving to the less fortunate

One of my dear friends, Billie, loves Christmas like I do! We have gotten together during this season for years. Once when we met she had a shopping bag full of little wrapped gifts! I asked, "What is in there?" She chuckled. "I'll show you!" Walking around, we saw many homeless and less fortunate and Billie took out the gift bags, which were filled with warm socks! The recipients were happy and we were too! Thus began a tradition. To add to the visual—Billie is tall and I am short—and we both wear mink coats! Picture this! Ho-ho-ho!

houses and opening safer ones, primarily for orphans. They also promoted programs for immigrants and the less fortunate, visiting orphans to help them celebrate Christmas with gifts and gaiety. When Roosevelt became the 26th President of the United States, Riis was invited to the White House and wrote, "Is There A Santa Claus?" This story is special because President Roosevelt then asked Riis what he wanted for Christmas. Riis asked him to send a telegram to his mother in Ribe, Denmark, which the President immediately did. So for Riis, Roosevelt was Santa Claus and was the source for the phrase "Santa Claus is the spirit of Christmas."

The renowned social reformer Riis also wrote numerous other Christmas books and articles to promote giving and charity. "Nibsy's Christmas" in 1893 graphically depicted the spirit of Christmas among the struggling residents of the Lower East Side tenements. Nibsy and other poor, young news carriers used their hard-earned money to buy presents for their friends and families. Many of Riis's meaningful Christmas writings are published in "Christmas Stories " (Macmillan, 1923), which can be bought online. Each year, I reread these sad yet joyful tales.

Riis also wrote about the TB Christmas Seal Program, which supported tuberculosis research and was started by a postal employee in his native Denmark. It inspired Ms. Emily Bissell in Delaware to begin a similar program in 1907 to sell TB seals like stamps, which became a long-standing tradition in the USA.

Knowing that many could not afford a Christmas tree, Riis also helped put up the first public tree in Madison Square Park in 1912, starting the worldwide tradition of public holiday trees and caroling.

IV

HERALDING THE SEASON!
MACY'S PARADE ON
THANKSGIVING EVE & DAY!

Gothamtide festivities begin when Macy's big balloons and falloons (the smaller ones) come to life on the closed off streets abutting The American Museum of Natural History on the vast block between 78th and 80th Streets, Central Park West and Amsterdam Avenue. Macy's started out as a fancy goods store in 1858. This renowned department store moved to its present location in 1901. The symbol of Macy's is a star, as its founder was a sailor first and inspired by the stars.

In 1924, the employees from many different nationalities proposed the idea of having a parade. Today Macy's employees from all over the country help by filling these balloons with helium and are busy with parade preparations not just all night but all year. Expertise in temperature and velocity is required to inflate these happy figures. A Macy's employee explained to me that each balloon has many compartments. If there is a confrontation with a tree, the wind or another obstacle, the whole balloon will not collapse but rather go limp, as we all have witnessed. *(You may feel limp too after all these revelries.)*

Each year new balloons are introduced, which take approximately three months to design and create. Some of the most popular are Snoopy, Mickey Mouse, Superman, SpongeBob Square Pants, Hello Kitty, and Felix the Cat. In 2014, I was thrilled when

my British friend Paddington Bear joined the parade. There are usually about twenty-seven balloons and of course, the American Favorite, Tom the Turkey.

The night before this special event has become popular and crowded, but it is fun to watch the balloons come "alive" and then be "bedded down" for the night on the street with lace-like ropes. In the morning when the balloons wake up for the parade, fifty linesmen or keepers are required to maneuver balloons on the parade route.

On Thanksgiving morning it is always exciting to watch the parade. In addition to the balloons, it includes approximately fourteen marching bands, thirty-two floats, one thousand cheerleaders, five hundred and thirty-eight clowns and crowds of cheering viewers lining the parade route from 80th Street to Macy's flagship store on Herald Square and 34th Street. (*Note: heralding in Herald Square - tis the season!*)

For several years I have helped out with the parade and am amazed that at 6 a.m. the route is already lined with eager parade watchers—some of whom have slept out all night. Last year I met some cheerleaders from Texas and they were so excited and honored to be heralding the start of the jolly and holly season. It is such fun! And when Santa Claus arrives at the end everyone knows that Gothamtide is here. Start celebrating! (*For more information about Macy's, see Fifth Avenue—Gothamtide Tour*).

V
ROCKEFELLER
CENTER

*I*n midtown Manhattan on Fifth Avenue between 48th and 51st Streets is the heart of Christmas and this booklet! As you stand on Fifth Avenue you will be dazzled by the panorama of Angels tooting their horns to welcome you to Rockefeller Center and the most famous Christmas tree in the world silhouetted against the soaring seventy story flagship skyscraper. Below The Tree waves the "golden gilded boy" Prometheus and the iconic ice skating rink. Isn't this one of the most spectacular sights you have ever seen? Twelve delicate wire angels—nine feet high with six-foot long long brass trumpets—herald your arrival as you stroll down the Channel Gardens decorated with greenery, which sits between the impressive French and British Empire buildings. An English woman, Valerie Clarebout, designed these graceful angels in 1954. *(Toot-toot!)*

In 1931 when Rockefeller Center was being built, the workers were so grateful to have jobs that they erected a tree to say "thank you" where the ice skating rink is now. John D. Rockefeller, Jr.—known as "Junior"—thought this was a noble idea and the first official Rockefeller Center tree went up in 1933 and began this magnificent tradition. I get excited every year when I walk down the Channel Gardens and see the decorations and The Tree *(or My Tree as I call it)*.

There is so much to see and do:

- ▲ Watch The Tree's arrival, decoration and lighting.
- ❀ See The Rockettes and the Christmas Spectacular.
- ▲ Be dazzled by all the Christmas decorations and events.
- ● View live camels walk around the block from Radio City.
- ▲ Stand out for NBC's Today Show and "Toys for Tots" gift-giving.
- ♪ Go Ice-skating at "the Pond." Opened in 1936, it was the first outdoor ice-skating rink in the U.S.
- ▲ Go to the Top of the Rock or the Rainbow Room to see New York City all lit up for Christmas —the colors are amazing.
- ▲ Savor all the splendid eateries in Rockefeller Center. Some are listed below. (Num-num!)
- ▲ Shop at the stores around Rockefeller Center and concourse below.
- 🎺 Listen to the Annual Tuba Concert on the second Sunday in December. *(see music listings)*.
- ▲ Spread Gothamtide spirit by smiling and talking to other merrymakers.

As The Spirited Elf, I have led tours of Rockefeller Center for many years and Christmas here is my favorite time. This is the center of "ho-ho-ho!"—joy, peace and hope—as you will see!

Let me tell you a bit about this majestic colossus, so that you can appreciate its importance. Rockefeller Center, a "city within a city," is the most important urban complex of the twentieth century. Built between 1931 and 1939 with later additions, it comprises about twenty buildings. John D Rockefeller, Jr. originally got involved with developing what became Rockefeller Center when he agreed to build a new complex for the Metropolitan Opera and was well along on this when the devastating

Great Depression of 1929 occurred. The MET project was terminated. A forward-thinking leader, Rockefeller attracted RCA/NBC as the flagship tenant and other communication companies followed. NBC is still at legendary 30 Rock! (Junior wanted to call his visionary undertaking Radio City but he was convinced that the name "Rockefeller Center" symbolized permanence and prestige!) Yes!!! Artists such as Paul Manship, Gaston Lachaise, Lee Lawrie and Hildreth Meière created about one hundred pieces of art and sculpture based on the themes of "The Progress of Man" and "New Frontiers." As you stroll around do look up at all the meaningful artwork. *(Plan to come on a tour with me sometime.)*

"Prometheus" is one of the most celebrated sculptures at Rockefeller Center. In Greek mythology, Prometheus brought fire to mankind. Designed by the highly regarded Paul Manship, this distinctive artwork at Rockefeller Center is reputed to be the most important sculpture in New York City after the Statue of Liberty. Prometheus looks contented between two stately trees. However, when he first arrived in 1934 a youth and a maiden—symbolic of the recipients of his gift of fire, flanked him. However, if you look at the entrance to the sunken plaza or ice rink at the bottom of the promenade, you will see these handsome bronze figures, which were moved here years ago and entice you to go ice skating or have a drink. Another great photo op! And behind them is a plaque imprinted with Junior Rockefeller's creed: "I believe in the supreme worth of the individual and in his right to life, liberty, and the pursuit of happiness." In the hubbub of Rockefeller Center stop and read the rest of his principles—a lasting Gothamtide gift!

Christmas was promoted in the 19th century with the growth of the printed word, newspapers and magazines, followed by radio and television. RCA (Radio Corporation of America) started the first national radio network in 1926. NBC (National Broadcasting Company) was owned by RCA until 1988, from then to 2015 by General Electric, then sold to Comcast, which is modernizing this landmark.

Rockefeller Center epitomizes the "Machine Age" with its many escalators, underground truck delivery docks, and the first indoor parking garage for automobiles. These streamlined designs used new building materials such as aluminum, stainless steel and other inventions such as air-cooling.

This magical mosaic is noteworthy for combining offices with restaurants, entertainment and shops. It was designed with an underground concourse to connect the buildings to the proposed subway and to provide additional space for stores, eateries,

restrooms and even a post office. Trees and other plantings create a year round, park-like setting because John D. Rockefeller, Jr. thought that nature should be included in the design. If you look up, you can see many terraces sprinkled among the buildings. Tenants and tourists can look down on greenery and open spaces. As you may guess, I am passionate about Rockefeller Center and delight in learning more. So do appreciate that this Rockefeller enthusiast is condensing so much information and knowledge into this small book.

The most exciting time is when the Christmas tree arrives. Part of the joy of Gothamtide at Rockefeller Center is sharing and learning about seasonal happenings with the Ambassador of Rockefeller Center, CJ Love. (And he is a love!) Standing outside 30 Rock on the plaza, he answers questions about anything to do with Rockefeller Center and more. *(If CJ isn't available, go into the glorious lobby with its intriguing artwork. At the reception desk a friendly concierge will assist you and there is printed information on Rockefeller Center and postcards of The Tree!)*

The Tree is chosen each year by photos submitted by tree lovers. Rock Center horticulturists also drive and fly around looking for trees. Send in a photo if you have a suggestion. As I travel around this country, I am always looking for suitable trees. One summer, I was in the tower of a historic house surrounded by trees on the Hudson River, when a small plane buzzed over us. Later we found out that this plane was looking for The Tree.

Here are some tree facts:

▲ In 1931 the first Tree erected by the workers was on the current site of the ice skating rink. Twenty feet tall, it was decorated with tin cans and garlands.

● In 1933 the first official Tree was 50-feet tall and decorated with seven hundred twinkling lights.

▲ In 1941 four live reindeer were part of the display and stayed in cages. (This wouldn't happen today!)

✪ The Tree must be a Norwegian spruce and at least 65-feet tall.

▲ In 1951 The Tree ceremony was on television for the first time featuring the famous singer, Kate Smith.

🎁 The farthest that The Tree ever came from was Ottawa, Canada in 1966, as part of the centennial celebration of the confederation of Canada.

▲ The tallest Tree was 100-feet tall to celebrate the 2000 Millennium and came from Connecticut.

★ The Trees are all between fifty to one hundred years old.

▲ Most of The Trees come from New York, New Jersey and Connecticut, but also from Pennsylvania.

▲ There are about 45,000 lights on The Tree, generated by solar panels on top of the big International building behind the statue of Atlas.

▲ In 1998 The Tree was flown in from Ohio but that was too dangerous and never repeated.

▲ Since 2004 Swarovski has created the spectacular 550-pound glistening star with 25,000 crystals on top of The Tree. On the plaza there is a replica of the star, information about how it is made, and charming crystal gifts.

▲ When The Tree is taken down in early January, some of the wood is used in houses built by Habitat for Humanity including sites in Brooklyn and Louisiana. (Maybe I should move so I can have The Tree with me all year?)

◍ The Boy Scouts from New Jersey also make mulch from some of the branches for New Jersey parks.

Once a tree is selected it is nourished for several months depending on its health. After it is cut down, it is girdled so the girth of The Tree can get through the bridges, tunnels and roads —an arduous task. Transporting it to Rockefeller Center on flatbed trucks is an enormous undertaking. Sometimes The Tree arrives on a barge. I look forward every year to watching it being delivered with CJ, my Rockefeller Center Ambassador. All during the season we share "Tree" stories. It is so exciting to watch a huge crane lift The Tree from the truck and then the process of erecting it. One year CJ banged the heavy spike into The Tree, which ends up securing The Tree to its stand. I was so proud of his strength. What an exciting role to play!

Once the soaring Tree is secured in place, a "tree-bird man" climbs up and throws lines to anchor it to 30 Rock and the ice skating rink. This is not an easy task when the wind is blowing or the weather is inclement. His name is Jimmy and he is such fun. Up in The Tree he makes bird noises—"caw, caw, caw"—a tradition that began the year that the Canadian tree arrived. When Mr. Tree Man climbed up The Tree a crow greeted him! It is very special to me as he always looks down and says, "Welcome to the Lady in Red."

CJ traditionally presents me with the first pinecone. I have a collection of them at home. It takes about two-and-a-half hours to get The Tree upright. It is amazing to see how fast the scaffolding goes up so that the workers can adjust the branches and put on the lights. This whole process takes several weeks. There is also a special salute when the huge, glittering 9-foot high Swarovski star is placed on the tippy top of The Tree.

Many unions work harmoniously on this Tree, but they all get along and love The Tree as I do! Many have been involved for years. One year a worker's granddaughter was very ill with cancer and a letter was put in The Tree for good luck. The child recovered, starting a tradition, which continues each year when a new letter is placed at the top.

I could regale you with so many meaningful stories about The Tree and also the folks who donate it. In 2010 a family from Mahopac, New York donated The Tree. A fireman, who was in the first truck that went in after 9/11, owned this house. Initially, his two children did not want to donate the tree but the parents explained how important sharing was and that it would be amazing to have their tree at Rockefeller Center for the entire world to see. The family found the original Christmas tree lights when they bought the house. How adorable and delightful these young children were as they took pride in sharing by handing out pieces of The Tree to tree-lovers like me.

"This tree is a gift to the world. I see it as a message of goodwill and peace on earth."
—David Murbach, former head gardener

Another year, a helicopter was looking for a tree around Trenton, New Jersey, and found some good candidates at a tree farm. The horticulturists landed their plane and found 2009's Christmas tree. The twin brothers who inherited the tree farm were thrilled as their late Hungarian mother and her husband bought the tree farm in 1931. She had nurtured a special Christmas tree over the years, feeding it with manure outside in summer and bringing it inside in winter until it was too big. She always said that someday this special tree would end up at Rockefeller Center and kept sending letters and photos. But nothing ever happened until the helicopter landed. It was very exciting to see the twin men realize that their mother's wish was coming to fruition. She also loved the bluebirds that once flocked to their tree farm but had disappeared after the growth of the Trenton corridor. Just before the tree was to make its journey to Manhattan the bluebirds came back! I just love this touching story!

In 2014, the eighty-second tree was from Hemlock, Pennsylvania, and donated by a young couple who bought their house because of the majestic tree. When Rock Center scouts approached them, they realized it was important to share the

splendor of their tree with everyone. At The Tree lighting the young donor was so vivacious and spoke to Tree enthusiasts like me. What is truly wonderful is that after I put her picture in my annual Gothamtide letter, a friend of mine in Princeton, New Jersey who received my epistle exclaimed that the young lady was the granddaughter of one

of her friends. So it was indeed special when Rachel, The Tree Lady, drove from Pennsylvania and I went down to Princeton from New York City so we could meet. We had a joyful reunion and dinner all because of the Rockefeller Center Christmas Tree. *(More magic!)*

LIGHTING OF THE TREE CEREMONY

*T*he Tree lighting ceremony takes place the week after Thanksgiving with live musical performances from 7– 9 pm, at Rockefeller Plaza, between West 49th and West 50th Streets and Fifth and Sixth Avenues.

The occasion is glitzy and glowing but very crowded. Tree fanciers start lining up in the morning. How fortunate I am that I work with NYCVP, the renowned full service travel company, and attend a celebratory lighting dinner and gala at Brasserie Ruhlmann, my favorite French restaurant adjacent to The Tree. On this festive eve, I enjoy talking to people who have stood out all day, creating camaraderie with our fellow merrymakers from all over the world. It is marvelous to make connections with friends and people with mutual interests while we savor the animated faces of children, watch the celebrated entertainers in magical scenes and sing carols spontaneously! (*"O Christmas Tree!"*)

What fun it is celebrating with three hundred guests from all over the world as we watch the entertainment on the plaza. How special to see all the dignitaries and listen to top performers and choral groups. The Rockettes kick for joy! There is such excitement when The Tree is lit. The Tree has about 45,000 lights and the impressive glittering Swarovski crystal star on top.

(Once when I was leaving the party some policemen that I didn't know gave me a brand new umbrella that someone had left behind. The spirit of Gothamtide is giving and I was the recipient!)

To celebrate the Gothamtide season at Rockefeller Center, here are two suggestions: If you want to avoid the merrymaking crowds, walk into the International Building on Fifth Avenue between 50th and 51st Streets, behind the huge sculpture of Atlas holding up the world and flanked by the two toy soldiers, at the entrance to the lobby. Savor the lobby then go down the escalator to the concourse with lots of shops, eateries and rest rooms. Take a left and you will be behind the ice skating rink, then take the escalator up to the lobby of the flagship building of Rockefeller Center—30 Rock. Go through the door and be dazzled: there is THE CHRISTMAS TREE!

Another picturesque way is to walk through the lobby of the International Building to the back and turn left to exit at the 50th Street door. What a splendiferous view with the garlands of glittering lights surrounding the plaza; The Tree, and below in the sunken plaza—Ice Skating rink, the Toy soldiers standing guard and Prometheus gleaming with joy at all the Gothamtide jollies!

You may be able to walk right over to The Tree, but if not, walk down 50th Street past The Tree, and the entrance to the Top of the Rock with its amazing Swarovski crystal chandelier and stairway; to the side entrance of 30 Rockefeller Center with the large neon sign on the marquee—"NBC Studios; Observation Deck and Rainbow Room." Go through the doors, turn left and walk through the magnificent lobby with poinsettias and murals on the walls. If you keep walking you will go through the revolving doors and there is Our Tree!!!! You may want to take in this splendiferous lobby where there is an information desk with more information on Rockefeller Center and postcards of The Tree.

The Tree lifts one's spirits for the whole year. CJ and I share experiences that we see and hear throughout the Christmas season.

> ▲ Year after year, I have given holiday tours to the same ladies from the Midlands in the U.K. who make an annual pilgrimage to see The Tree and the Gothamtide glories of New York City.

★ Every year CJ is asked to take photos, which include proposals and weddings. I will never forget one year when a poor bride got married in sleeting snow.

▲ Once CJ and I were standing by The Tree when someone asked, "Where is the tree?" Good grief! It was in front of them.

✪ Someone else once asked if The Tree was artificial and stood on the plaza all year long.

▲ What joy it brought to an 8-year-old when I sang "Happy Birthday" to him followed by "Jingle Bells." Everyone joined in!

🎁 Whenever we hear cheering from the ice skating rink, we know that it is another engagement. (One can rent the ice skating rink and get champagne for an engagement). In essence, The Tree lifts one's spirits! And so does the Tuba Concert!

In 1974, the Tuba master and musician Harvey Phillip from Indiana University proposed the idea of a Tuba Concert on the ice skating rink and this has become a tradition, not only at

Rockefeller Center but in many states and even abroad. Hundreds of tuba and euphonium players, both young and old, gather for this on the concourse before performing on the ice skating rink. One player brings his tuba from Australia. I have met many of the tuba players from around the country and have even recruited some players. *So blow on merrily!*

Beneath The Tree is a concourse with many festive places to buy gifts, food or find a place to sit or restrooms. Go skating or look at the skaters. There are table and chairs so relax and take in the bustling holiday!

Let's scurry down the street to see The Rockettes at Radio City. On the way, stop to view the creative windows at Anthropologie, a store on 50th Street at Rockefeller Plaza. Recently all the windows on both the plaza and concourse level featured charming gingerbread houses and cakes. Look at the end of the Plaza at 51th street all aglow with The American Girl store full of holiday happenings, presents, and events. A treat for all ages including Queen Santa.

"The Tree makes me happy; lifts my spirits upward; is cool; awesome; makes kids out of all of us and is a symbol of the peace and joy that the season should bring."

At the end of the block is **Radio City Music Hall,** the first building to open at Rockefeller Center in December 1932. I get so excited thinking about the annual "Radio City Christmas Spectacular" with thirty-six kicking Rockettes making frequent costume changes, a mighty Wurlitzer organ, dancing bears, Mr. and Mrs. Santa Claus, ice skaters on a tiny rink that appears from below, and a real bus on the stage! The finale is the majestic and sacred "Nativity Scene" with live sheep, a donkey and several camels. The animals stay at Radio City during the spectacular. I still chuckle at the story an orchestra member once told me

about the stubborn camel that refused to budge from the center of the stage. The orchestra in front kept playing, "We Three Kings of Orient Are." Finally the camel lifted its leg and sprayed the orchestra! So bring a Kleenex!

If you want to see the camels, come to Rock Center early in the morning when they go for their morning constitutional around the block. In fact, I had my picture taken with them before I was on NBC TV to talk about Christmas. *(Oh bliss!)*

As you may have guessed by now, I love talking about architecture and buildings. Radio City is one of the best examples of the Art Deco style, designed by Edward Durell Stone with interiors by Donald Deskey. Take a tour of this jazz age landmark. The soaring lobby features the commanding mural, "The Fountain of Youth" by Ezra Winter. Do you know that this mural was so filthy from nicotine and dirt stains that twenty restorers used "Q-tips" to clean it? If you have time go to the top floor and walk down to check out the grandeur, statues and different views. Look at the chandeliers and lighting fixtures. Don't forget to peek into the restrooms as they have interesting art and Art Deco pieces. And take in the lower level too with noteworthy art and period furnishings also in the men's room.

Radio City is also noteworthy because the stage can be moved up and down. In fact, during World War II the Federal Government came in to study its unique engineering. So many Radio City fanciers go in the side doors on 50th and 51st Streets, but be sure to look on top of the marquee on Avenue of the Americas (or Sixth Avenue), to see the dazzling Christmas tree. I always admire the three splendid medallions on the 50th Street side of Radio City which illustrate "Song, Dance and Drama" by the noted sculptor and mosaicist, Hildreth Meière, a talented

woman who is now finally being appreciated. (Thank heavens all her records, photos and diaries were kept by her daughter and granddaughter, resulting in the award-winning book, "The Art Deco Murals of Hildreth Meière," published in 2014.)

Across Sixth Avenue from Radio City are the Rockefeller Center newer buildings with more Gothamtide displays. To the left are big Christmas ornamental balls and Christmas lights on the plazas. Right across from Radio City is a toy train that goes back and forth on its track and toots! Children love to watch this train. In keeping with the theme of the Parade of the Wooden Soldiers at Radio City, one block north on Sixth Avenue at the entrance to the **1285 Avenue of the Americas Art Gallery**, large toy wooden soldiers stand guard and another photo opportunity!

GOTHAMTIDE ALL YEAR LONG
AT ROCKEFELLER CENTER

I happily discovered that Gothamtide is at Rockefeller Center all year long. Walk into the side entrance of the International Building on 50th Street, past the reception desk to the farthest passageway. Take a right and walk toward Fifth Avenue and on the way observe the well-designed elevators together with the multi-colored and patterned green marble from Tinos, Greece. What a pleasant surprise I had one day while gazing up at the marble panels. In the left-hand panel, around the entrance doors, I saw a row of Christmas trees at the tippy top beneath the golden ceiling. Below, I visualized a man's face, angels, a bear, and even Christmas ornaments. Since this imaginative awakening, I ask folks on my tours to look up and we all have fun. Sightings include Father Christmas, some fish, Christ, and an Indian chief. These figures are not planned but are variations in the marble. Come and see!

Walk out the front doors on Fifth Avenue where the mighty statue of Atlas holds up the world and St. Patrick's Cathedral beckons you all year long!

When thinking about Gothamtide, I go to this spectacular lobby year round to look at the Christmas tree and angels. Another place to feel Gothamtide at Rockefeller Center is in front of the flagship building 30 Rockefeller Center on the plaza. On the site of the Christmas tree is a circular, bronze medallion in the ground, which says "Christmas Tree—Rockefeller Center." I chuckle as so many walk over this while in awe of the plaza, its flags, artwork and the whole scene. So if possible I point out this memorable medallion, which is sacred ground to many of us! Use your imagination—look up and around! Be inspired by Rockefeller Center. May the spirit of Gothamtide continue for you all year and. Here's to hope, peace and enlightenment!!

Cuisine

Brasserie Ruhlmann faces the plaza off Fifth Avenue and 50th Street. My favorite eatery at Rockefeller Center all year long. At Christmas, this is where I am fortunate to attend the lighting of My Tree where they call me Queen Santa.

Weather permitting, some years the patio outside is open for drinks and a delicious meal. If not, enjoy the resplendent interior honoring the famous French Art Deco designer, Emile-Jacques Ruhlmann. From inside you can look out at My Tree! Year round, I love to sit on their outdoor patio at night and take in the beautiful lights and grandeur of the most important urban complex of the 20th century. Adjacent to the Ice skating rink with great views of the skaters and the golden boy Prometheus are:

- **The Sea Grill** with excellent fish

- **Rock Center Cafe** where you can have breakfast with Santa, lunch and other meals all day.

- On the concourse are many eateries including **Starbucks.**

- For an elevated treat go to the zenith of **30 Rock** and **The Rainbow Room** for spectacular views of all the holiday lights and have a drink and or a meal in this jazz age legend.

- **21 Club** at 21 West 52nd Street is my other favorite eatery in the Rockefeller Center area. The jockeys on the outside welcome you and the fresh greens draping the gates smell Christmas-y. Have a hot toddy and their renowned chicken hash! Look for the "Lady in Red" on Christmas Eve caroling with the Salvation Army. "Oh come all ye faithful." *(see Fifth Avenue — Gothamtide Tour)*

★ Note the bas relief in **Brasserie Ruhlmann** inspired by the "Normandie" ship by Artgroove's Ronald Genereux and Hank Richards.

VI
FIFTH AVENUE—
GOTHAMTIDE LANE
TOUR

Join Queen Santa on this spirited stroll to see some of the legendary Christmas displays! *(Dress warmly and wear comfortable shoes)*

Seeing the windows, storefronts and decorations change each year is one of the most exhilarating and bountiful Gothamtide treats. I am providing a lot of detail on renowned stores and other treats with street numbers on your left and right, but refer to other location maps too. It's really not that complicated. Just walk, look at the windows, turn the corners, find surprises, and look up at the holiday ornaments, beasties and architectural elements. I recommend looking at store displays all year long, as some are so creative and inspiring.

Before heading to Gothamtide Lane, stroll up Madison Avenue to 60th Street and look at the festive store windows in **Barneys**, a chic New York store, known for its inventive and dazzling holiday displays. The theme—"Chilling Out" had an "ice" theme! One window featured the famous glassmaker, Dale Chihuly's, Winter Brilliance star. People were glued to another window, watching ice craftsmen carving huge ice blocks into penguins and other creatures. *(Brrrh! So glad to be wearing my trusty red coat!)*

Stroll over a few blocks to the Neo-Gothic **Arsenal Building** on 64th Street and Fifth Avenue inside Central Park. For over thirty years the headquarters of the NYC Department of Parks and Recreation has held an exhibition of Christmas wreaths in the third floor gallery. *(Yes, the Arsenal was originally built to store explosives in the 1850s before Central Park was created).* This world famous park, designed by Frederick Law Olmsted and Calvert Vaux from 1858–1876, is a treasure trove. Go behind the Arsenal to the **Central Park Zoo** to wish the sea lions a merry Gothamtide. And you can visit the zoo to see many animals like monkeys, bees, birds and penguins. (One year after my Rockefeller Center Tree came down some of its limbs were brought to the zoo for a special workshop for children to imaginatively paint the pieces. I still have one!!)

To the right of the sea lions, look up at the Delacorte musical animal clock, conceived by and donated by publisher and philanthropist George Delacorte in 1965. Medieval bell towers on town halls and churches inspired him and the Italian sculptor Andrea Spadini crafted these bronze animals. Every hour and half hour the bear, elephant, monkeys, a goat, penguin and kangaroo parade around and play carols like "Deck the Halls" and "Hark, the Herald Angels Sing" during December. How fortunate I've been to hear "Jingle Bells," while the animals dance around the clock, and how often I've appreciated this spectacular zoo. Walk under the clock to the Children's Zoo, which is a delight too, as is the whole park.

Walk down the park road a few blocks and welcome to Fifth Avenue, which I call Gothamtide Lane. This is called **Grand Army Plaza**. Across is the commanding statue of General William Tecumseh Sherman, the noted Civil War general, by the renowned sculptor Augustus Saint-Gaudens. One knows that Sherman will win the battle, as the golden lady statue of Nike, the symbol of victory, is leading him. In front of this statue is a Menorah, a huge branched candlestick, a symbol of Judaism and Hannukah. It's a New York City tradition to watch The Festival of Lights as the candles are lit on eight nights to celebrate Hannukah. On your left you will see lots of people on the plaza between 58th and 59th Streets going in and out of the busiest Apple Store in New York with the iconic cube. On the south side of Grand Army Plaza you will see the sculptor Karl Bitter's stunning statue of Pomona, the goddess of abundance, pouring water symbolically into the many-layered fountain. At Christmas tiny decorated trees surround the Pulitzer Fountain, donated by publisher Joseph

Pulitzer in 1916. On the west side of the plaza between 58th and 59th Streets is Eloise's home! "Let's go!"

The holiday feeling picks up even more when you go into the legendary and elegant **Plaza Hotel** (Henry Hardenbergh, 1903-1905), which contains the Christmas spirit of Eloise! A stately Christmas tree greets you and then you can luxuriate with high tea in the historic Palm Court. Wish Eloise's portrait a "Merry Gothamtide" and think about what you want for Christmas when you visit a real Santa Claus nearby. Then scurry down the escalator to a splendid array of eateries and shops, but most importantly the Eloise Store. Special teas can be arranged here too. I just love this store and am always buying special gifts for all my friends and many godchildren, who also learned to love Eloise from the time that they could walk. How did Eloise do her shopping? Eloise would call a shop and say, "Will you kindly send over a little petit quelque chose and have it gift wrapped for me Eloise? And charge it please and thanks a lot."

One day I sat down on the plush pillows and happened to watch the delightful movie "Eloise at the Plaza" (TV Movie 2003) with Julie Andrews. *(A great treat!)*

Across the street from the Plaza and behind the statue of Pomona is stately **Bergdorf Goodman** at 754 Fifth Avenue, another New York City specialty store famous for its Christmas display. One year these windows depicted "Brilliant Holiday" with over seven million Swarovski crystals embedded in the displays. The details depicted in these gem-filled windows are overwhelming, including rock stars and a monkey telling fortunes. One must study these windows carefully to appreciate the workmanship. How fortunate I was one night when one of the designers saw me studying the windows. He stopped to explain the intricate work involved in arranging these small crystals into patterns. *(Gothamtide Spirit again!)* Often the crowds are pushy, so do come early in the morning or later in the evening. And be sure to look across at Bergdorf's festive men's windows.

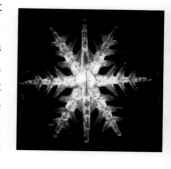

Blink at the bling! At the corner of 57th Street, look up at the monumental Snowflake, an "outdoor chandelier" with 16,000 Baccarat crystals holding court in the middle of the street. Weighing 3000 pounds, this revered icon is 28-feet tall and 23-feet wide replacing the original snowflake from 1984. Created by lighting designer, Ingo Maurer for UNICEF in 2002, this magnificent beacon is a symbol of hope, peace and compassion for the children of the world. I hope it enlightens you too! If you want to have your name engraved on one of the crystals contact UNICEF!

On 57th Street to your left and right are many stores. **Burberry,** the British shop, had the only window that I could find that included Santa Claus in its holiday display in 2015. To your right, note the candy canes hanging from a skyscraper. 57th Street is now being called Billionaire Row because of all the soaring glass towers. Stroll over two blocks west to check out or attend a Christmas concert at **Carnegie Hall** (William Tuthill, 1891), at 881 7th Ave at West 57th Street. I just love the sound and ambiance of the many different historic concerts including numerous "Messiahs," the New York Pops and the adorable Vienna Boys Choir. These definitely will get you fa-la-laing!

Continue to look up at the storefronts on your left and right on 57th Street bedecked with glittering jeweled necklaces. **Tiffany & Co.**, the renowned jewelry and gift store, has charming gem-box windows with classical elements including little reindeer. A few years ago, **Bulgari,** another elegant jewelry store across from Tiffany's, mounted their company's symbol, the serpent, lighting up the corner of their building. Everyone loved this glistening animal swirling at the corner. That year Tiffany had their traditional elegant holiday windows. However, the next year Tiffany also draped its exterior with a glittering necklace. I wonder what will happen this year?

Next to Tiffany is **Trump Tower,** which has a big tree in their lobby. Also take the escalator up and down to shops, Starbucks, and places to sit.

Across 56th Street, the elegant jeweler **Harry Winston's** vintage town house is ablaze with glittering diamonds. Next door, **Henri Bendel** has an interior tree adorned with gifts.

Some of the most creative windows all year long are across the street at the famed Italian boutique, **Dolce & Gabanna**. Christmas angels adorn a classical and intricate chapel door. There is an elegant and bountiful Christmas table with lots of festive gourmet treats.

On the south side of 55th Street are two stately hotels symbolic of the Gilded Age. To your left, The **St. Regis's** lobby is decorated with Santa's sleigh and flowers. There is also a Christmas boutique that sells interesting gifts. Across Fifth Avenue you can see a cluster

of glittering deer atop the canopy welcoming you to the **Peninsula Hotel**. What a joy to walk into their elegant lobby adorned with Christmas greens and snowmen. Look at the exquisite tree by the elevators. This hotel has the Christmas spirit, as every weekend carolers perform amid the special decorations. Such warm and thoughtful staff! Once I brought one of my little friends, Anthony, aged 7, who was awed by the lights and snowmen. A staff member appeared with a goodie bag filled with sweets, a Santa Claus and an ornament. On my tours I take the merrymakers into the hotel to hear the caroling groups on the weekends. Everyone loves this treat! We all sing along—a true testament of the Gothamtide spirit!

Back across Fifth Avenue peek into **Coca-Cola**'s lobby with a mounted display of vintage "Santa Claus" ads by Haddon Sundblom. A talented illustrator, he created ads showing Santa Claus savoring a Coke for over thirty years from 1931 to 1964, and is credited with making the 20th century "jolly Santa Claus" image. Does pausing here making you feel refreshed as Coke says?

Across the street at 54th Street, **Gap** has a special message: "do something good today." How fitting for this season and all year long!

At 53rd Street, is the magnificent Gothic Revival Church, **Saint Thomas Church Fifth Avenue,** home of the renowned Saint Thomas Choir of Men and Boys. After a fire ruined the previous building, the architects, Cram and Goodhue, completed this highly acclaimed Episcopal Church in 1913. Saint Thomas is known worldwide for its outstanding choral music. At Gothamtide two Handel's "Messiahs," Benjamin Britten's "Ceremony of Carols" and John Rutter's "Dancing Day" are heralded. The music is spectacular and the boys are my size. I love watching and smiling at the boys! In fact, walk in now to take in the beauty of this church with its spectacular carved reredos, depicting different religious and political figures, and just relax. Perhaps you will hear the choristers practicing. These young boys and gentlemen sing frequently at the 5pm Evensong weekday services. (Fa-la-la!) Attending their famous Christmas Eve service is inspirational and perhaps you will see the Lady in Red! Bells ring, the organ resonates, an orchestra plays and the Saint Thomas Choir of Men and Boys sing.

This service and the one at Saint Patrick's Cathedral a few blocks south are two of the most acclaimed Christmas Eve services. Tickets are available only for parishioners, so to attend

one must go early and stand in line for several hours. It is definitely worth it! Or call for tickets—perhaps you will be lucky!

Walk down Gothamtide Lane a block to 52nd Street, take a right and a short distance down the street you will see a vintage brownstone adorned with fragrant boxwood and thirty-five jockeys saluting you—"**21 Club**." This famed "speakeasy," built in 1872, has a lovely Gothamtide custom and the friendliest staff. In 1938, on a cold, snowy Christmas evening the owners, Jack and Charlie, stepped outside and found the Salvation Army per-

forming seasonal music. They kindly invited them in to warm up and enjoy some hot food. As a thank you, the Salvation Army musicians started playing Christmas carols thus creating a lovely and lasting tradition. This Christmas event has become so popular, partly spurred on by Queen Santa's praise (Ha!), that there are now lunch-

eons and dinners in December culminating in a special Christmas Eve performance. One of my favorite things to do during the season, the Gothamtide spirit gets energized with caroling, donating to the Salvation Army and enjoying the special, historic ambiance and cuisine of the famous 21 Club. *(Fa-la-la!)*

Next door, check out **Paley Center for Media** (The Museum of Television and Radio), which features Christmas classics in Paleyland dressed for the season including Santa and cocoa too!" One can also do research and look up many media interests.

There are so many turnovers in New York City real estate with changing times, escalating costs and demands. Many existing stores are forced out when the rent becomes too costly. In the interim, some building owners have "pop-up" stores to garnish quick income until the space is rented. Recently **Lands' End** had a "pop-up" store at 52nd Street and Fifth Avenue. When you walked in the door, the aroma of cocoa and holiday spices was soothing. Upstairs, generous Lands' End had free samples of cocoa together with peppermint and caramel cookies! *(What a treat! And it was a treat to tell Christmas fanciers too. Thank you Lands' End!)*

Across the street is **Cartier's**, the last remaining Beaux-Arts mansion from the Gilded Age on Fifth Avenue, dating from 1905. Step back in time and visualize Fifth Avenue when it was once lined with similar opulent mansions. As New York City grew and the population kept moving further uptown, the area became more commercial. This architecturally significant dwelling with some of its original interiors became home to Cartier's, the French jeweler, in 1914. After an extensive restoration, be sure to go to the top floor and walk down the graceful winding staircase with noteworthy artwork and gifts. At Christmas the whole house is tied up with an enormous, festive red bow. The store windows are filled with incredible jewels in creative window box displays. *(Note that at night the jewels are removed and you can understand why!)* Under a canopy of greens, Christmas music is piped out to the sidewalk for merrymakers to enjoy.

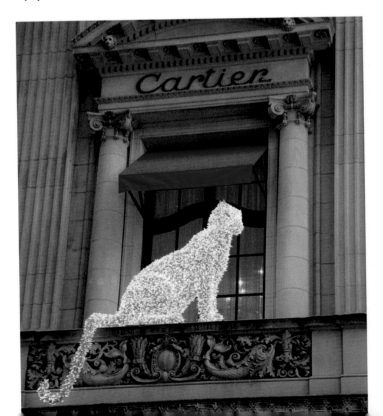

The spires of **Saint Patrick's Cathedral,** between 50th and 51st Streets, loom above. This towering cathedral, completed in 1878, faced problems some years ago as chunks of limestone were falling from the facade and the stained glass windows were being eroded. In 2015, the extensive restoration was completed in time for Pope Francis's visit. "St. Pat's" is an important and beloved destination for visitors to New York City. There are numerous concerts and my favorite at Christmas is "New York Sings," with many different musical groups including the Young People's Chorus, composed of young folks from all over New York City. This award-winning choral group has performed at the lighting of the Rockefeller Center Tree across the street. Their founder has taken them on foreign tours and they have performed at the White House. Part of my job as Gothamtide's Queen Santa is to discover other groups like this, and I often go to concerts at various venues, like the 92nd Street Y.

Besides the plethora of Christmas concerts featuring music from many different countries, Christmas is really celebrated at St. Pat's with a magnificent crèche scene with life size figures (if you are petite like me). Nativity scenes have traditionally included animals. In 2011, Italian sculptors working at St. Patrick's and the Rector, Monsignor Robert T. Ritchie used his dog as a model and a new figure was added to the crèche scene— a dog! *(Arf - arf! Very appropriate in this "doggy age." New York City is a dog-loving place but don't trip over the leashes.)*

Across 51st Street the huge glass skyscraper **Olympic Tower** has a relaxing lobby with plaster casts from the Parthenon in Greece, occasional music, fantastic exhibits and comfortable seating. *(A special place!)*

Walk around St. Patrick's Cathedral, which spans a whole block. At the corner of 50th Street and Madison Avenue is the **Cardinal's Residence.** (Often there are lights on and I wonder if he is looking out at us or at the Italian Renaissance-styled mansion across the street and thinking of Rome).

The mansion with a courtyard is the **Lotte New York Palace Hotel,** a perfect example of an Italian palace or palazzo right here in Manhattan. This handsome row was built from 1882 to 1886 as six separate residences joined by a common façade. In the courtyard, look at the enormous, beautifully decorated tree. Walk around for the best place to take a magnificent photo of the tree with the sculptural St. Patrick's Cathedral outlined in the background and 30 Rockefeller Center glowing in the distance.

Look up at the notable Gilded Age interiors of the Villard House on the south side of the courtyard. (Hopefully, this will again be a chic eatery!) You can walk through the lobby to warm up or have refreshment. Lotte just took over the Palace Hotel, so their Christmas plans are not known, but I have a feeling that Gothamtide will be there.

Across from Rockefeller Center, between 49th and 50th

Streets, is **Saks Fifth Avenue**, the well-known department store, which opened in 1924 and is acclaimed for its Christmas window displays. In recent years Saks has displayed a dazzling, show-stopping presentation called "The Palace" on its facade with streaming LED lights and music. Coupled with the popularity of Rockefeller Center, the crowds are overwhelming as visitors appreciate this colorful display—a fantastically illuminated silhouette of a palace with turrets bathed in changing blue lights. At intervals Christmas music such as, "We Wish You a Merry Christmas," emanates from this luminous palace with icy store windows, featuring glamorous women and the Taj Mahal.

Saks' interior at Christmas is also festive. Their beautiful columns are abundantly decorated with glittering greens and in the center an elevated display includes charming Art Deco-styled deer. The ground floor is filled with perfume displays. I love to go in and have a few sprays. This is how I discovered Jo Malone, which has such natural fragrances.

Walking down Fifth Avenue on 44th street go west a few blocks to bustling Times Square. **Gulliver's Gate** at 216 West 44th Street is a wonderland of miniature models and vignettes from around the world. Try to find Santa riding his sleigh in the sky.

Below 42nd Street is the noteworthy Beaux-Arts building, the **New York Public Library**, which takes up the two blocks. I just love the grandeur of the architecturally significant library, completed in 1911 by Carrere and Hastings, and its joyful Christmas spirit. The famed, recumbent lions welcome visitors, dressed for the season with their wreaths. Unfortunately, one year a Scrooge stole one wreath. New York City Mayor Fiorello La Guardia named the lions Patience and Fortitude *(Yes, the airport is named for him!)* in the 1930s to exemplify the attributes needed to live through The Great Depression. How appropriate as patience and fortitude are what we merrymakers need to survive the Christmas crush! Inside the lobby has a soaring Christmas tree. And many seasonal events take place here. The gift shop is full of thoughtful and unique gifts. *(Treat yourself!)*

"I will honor Christmas in my heart and try to keep it all the year."

— Charles Dickens

Behind the library is **Bryant Park** with **Bank of America's "Winter Village,"** which includes a superb decorated tree of approximately forty feet, and a European-inspired Christmas market with 125 boutiques, unique gifts, entertainment and eateries. The French carousel is particularly delightful. There is a free ice skating rink, but one must pay to rent skates. In the true Christmas spirit, the Winter Village began giving awards in 2002, as part of a special event to honor young people who have done positive things.

A few blocks down Fifth Avenue between 38th and 39th Streets is **Lord & Taylor,** another renowned department store known for historically-inspired holiday displays. Lord & Taylor is supposedly the oldest luxury store in the U.S., founded in 1826. As the population moved uptown, so did Lord & Taylor, and this location was completed in 1914. These intricately designed, creative windows with multiple moving parts are assembled below in elevators and then hydraulically raised into place. Like other major Christmas displays in the city, it takes all year to conceive and develop these animated windows. Lord & Taylor was also the first store to not have merchandise for sale in their holiday windows. A rarity these days! This past year "The Favorite Treats" theme featured amazing gingerbread houses, incorporating adorable little gingerbread figures. What a thrill for me when at the unveiling of the Christmas windows, "Santa Claus" spotted my red coat and we bonded immediately, discussing the many joys of Christmas while listening to carolers. Recently, Lord & Taylor erected an outdoor canopy covered with greenery and supplied with heating lamps for the season. It makes waiting in line and viewing their windows a much warmer experience. (*How thoughtful!*)

To see the original autographed copy of Charles Dickens' "A Christmas Carol," scamper over to **The Morgan Library and Museum** at Madison Avenue and 33 East 36th Street to the home of J.P. Morgan, the illustrious financier and collector.

Yes, this stately Italianate palace (Charles McKim, 1906) with a modern section is a museum. Each Christmas, a different page is shown. While there, check out his stately library, other exhibits, holiday events and superb gift store.

The iconic **Empire State Building** (1931) soars above 34th Street. Did you know this was the tallest building in the world at 1250 feet, until the former Twin Towers grew to 1350 feet in 1973? Its spire is illuminated red and green during the holiday. So many people just go to the top and never see the handsome Art Deco interior. There are always Christmas displays in the lobby, and at times Christmas music fills the air from a pianist tickling the ivories. Do go up to the top of the Empire State Building to see the spectacular views of the city and festive lights. Be certain to look out for Santa Claus and his sleigh!

From the Empire State Building, it is one block west to Broadway to visit the internationally famous and acclaimed Macy's Department Store—a miracle on 34th Street!

MACY'S—THE
CHRISTMAS STORE

R.H. Macy opened his "fancy dry goods store" at Sixth Avenue and 14th Street in 1858. As business boomed, it moved to the present location in Herald Square at 34th Street in 1902, expanding over time to become the world's largest department store.

Macy's had the first Christmas windows in 1882 and they were adorned with imported dolls. Street lighting changed shopping habits as people strolled around looking at stores and displays. A live Santa Claus (*shh!*) appeared at about the same time. Macy's has many Christmas customs, including a theme of "I Believe." When you walk along 34th Street the enormous figure of Virginia ("*Yes, Virginia there is a Santa Claus*" as described more fully in the History of Christmas chapter) on the canopy welcomes you.

Virginia's story is beautifully and creatively told in the windows on 34th Street as well. Macy's store windows on Broadway between 34th and 35th are always intricate and festive. Charlie Brown was the theme one year. Each year the windows become more tech savvy. Now they are interactive and one can ask questions.

Be sure to go inside the ground floor, which is a winter wonderland. Look up, as even the columns have festive holiday displays. In the middle of the floor is a huge "Believe in the art of giving" display and mailbox. Blank letters to Santa Claus, and pens are provided. For each letter that is put in the big "Santa" mailbox with Virginia, Macy's gives a contribution to "Make A Wish" foundation. I fill out several letters to Santa Claus, but instead of asking for something my messages express giving and gratitude!

Take the elevator up to Macy's legendary Santaland where the jolly man is. It is fun to go up to see Santa but be prepared for the long lines unless you make a special reservation. There are many festive displays in Santaland and great gifts throughout the store. Vignettes of former Christmas windows, like "A Miracle on Thirty-Fourth Street" are on view.

VII
PARK AVENUE TO
GRAND CENTRAL

*A*nother inspiring thing to do is to walk over two blocks from My Tree at Rock Center to Park Avenue on 52nd or 53rd Street to look at the **"Parade of Lighted Trees"** on the center islands from 54th Street up to 96th Street. This glowing tradition of illuminated trees was started in 1945 when a grieving mother wanted to commemorate her brave son and others killed in World War II.

On the first Sunday of December, the **Brick Presbyterian Church** at 91st Street and Park Avenue holds the lighting ceremony. Taps is played and carols are sung. When a switch is pulled, the lights go on sequentially in the symmetrically placed trees down Park Avenue. Although green, red and white lights were commonplace, white lights are used for symbolic reasons and to not confuse the taxi drivers!

Between 52nd and 53rd Streets is a mini-forest of about 350 little trees adorned with tiny white lights in front of the iconic **Seagram Building** completed in 1958. Mies van der Rohe designed the exterior and the acclaimed interiors are by Philip Johnson. The noted designer, Gene Moore, also of Tiffany, created this holiday display to complement the adjacent glittering commemorative trees across the street. This was the first use of small white lights that have become so popular. (It is such fun to explore and discover these factual tidbits!)

Walking down Park Avenue a few blocks you will see an imposing church, **St. Bartholomew's**, between 50th and 51st Streets (Bertram Goodhue, 1919). This Episcopal Church has an interesting history as the whole entrance was moved from its former location on Madison Avenue and 24th Street (Stanford White, 1902). Look carefully at the entrance columns with tired looking beastie lions. *(But wouldn't you be if you were holding up a column?)* Observe all the religious figures, rosettes, and other decorations on this spectacular entrance. The interior has many interesting design features crafted by Lee Lawrie and Hildreth Meière, who created noteworthy art for Rockefeller

Center too. Walk down the right aisle and see if you can find the Nativity scene in one of the capitals. In an annex hall, a space large enough for Christmas pageants, is a tasty eatery "Inside the Park." Check out their noteworthy Gothamtide music.

In the next block is the famous **Waldorf Astoria Hotel** (Schultze & Weaver, 1931). This elegant Art Deco landmark used to have superb Christmas displays of old holiday celebrations. At the entrance, look at the flagpoles held up by vintage eagles. (Sadly, the Waldorf is being modernized and the Gothamtide role is uncertain.) In 1982, cherry and hawthorn trees were added on a few blocks in the vicinity of the Waldorf Astoria Hotel to commemorate Hannukah.

At 230 Park Avenue is the towering former **New York Central Railroad Building** (Warren & Wetmore, 1929), former headquarters of the train company that built Grand Central. It used to be part of the "Parade of Lighted Trees" on Park Avenue, when lights in some of the window formed a cross. Times have changed and now colorful, changing floodlights illuminate the façade! Gaze up at the tower on top of the building with many figures including Mercury and some buffaloes—since one of the trains ended up in Buffalo, New York. This unique building has arched portals for cars and people. Look up Park Avenue with all the commemorative lights that lift up our lives.

Walk through to 44th Street, cross over to the modern **MetLife Building**, continue walking to the escalators and go down to the magical **Grand Central Terminal**. Whitney Warren described the architecture of this Beaux Arts landmark

as a "triumphant portal" to New York. This space is amazing! Gaze up at the blue ceiling graced with the constellations of the zodiac. Guess what—they are upside down but still ethereal! Sometimes at Gothamtide the starscape on the ceiling is illuminated. Can you pick out any constellations? So many spontaneous singing and planned Christmas events have occurred in this space. To the right is the **New York Transit Museum**, which has special holiday displays of vintage trains. If you are interested in trains, this is a must! *(Toot-toot!)* A great place for gifts too, together with all the shops and eateries in Grand Central, which is really grand. One of the best-known Christmas markets takes place here in **Vanderbilt Hall,** which used to be the waiting room for the trains. Reminder—if you haven't seen the rats scurrying up the lines of the canopy of the **Graybar Building**, go out to Lexington Avenue, take a left and look up!

Step out onto 42nd Street and Park Avenue and walk a few blocks south to get a good view of Grand Central's Classical facade with the huge clock, some spectacular statues of Roman gods and an eagle. *(It is jolly to explore and discover these soaring statues and little tidbits!).*

Cuisine

There are many good establishments spread throughout the terminal. The legendary **Oyster Bar**, which opened in 1913, is the place for oysters and fish dishes. Walk down the ramp to the entrance of this historic eatery. Outside the entrance, look up at the intricate patterned tiles in the ceiling. *(Guastavino invented these lighter tiles in 1885).* If you stand in the corners and speak softly, others can hear you across the space. This "whisper" gallery is melodious!

Healthy Danish food is taking over Grand Central with the **Great Northern Food Hall,** by Claus Meyer, whose Noma restaurant in Copenhagen is considered one of the best in the world. The Food Hall opened in part of Vanderbilt Hall to rave reviews in the summer of 2016, and has many stations serving nutritious food and tables to sit at too. The open-faced sandwiches, pastries and everything else are nummy. If you enter Grand Central from 42nd and Vanderbilt Avenue you will see the "hot dog" stand (recently voted the best in New York) and the upscale "Agern" restaurant.

VIII
UPPER EAST SIDE

One of the most spectacular places in New York City is **The Metropolitan Museum of Art** at Fifth Avenue and 82nd Street. This Beaux-Arts colossus in a ceremonial site adjacent to Central Park possesses one of the finest and most diverse art collections in the world. Walking up the steps look at the commanding columns with the four caryatids representing Painting, Sculpture, Architecture, and Music and lion gargoyles at intervals along the cornices. *(Are the lions smiling or yawning?)*

I often take young friends to the Met. There is so much to see and learn. One godchild said this museum "is like a candy shop which has so many selections to taste." At Christmas, the tasty treat is the angel-bedecked, soaring Christmas tree.

Once you get your tickets walk directly back (towards the rear of the museum facing Central Park) weaving through many collections and statues. Walk into a large chapel-like room with lots of statues and sculpture. This twenty-foot, beautifully decorated tree in the medieval sculpture hall is such an impressive sight. Standing in front of an 18th century Spanish choir screen with delicate ironwork from the Cathedral of Valladolid in Spain, with piped-in Christmas music, adds to this memorable setting. A Neapolitan crèche and tree are adorned with two hundred

18th century figures. How fortunate for The Met to have these gifts donated by Loretta Hines Howard in 1957. Her mother gave her a Neapolitan angel for her marriage in Chicago in 1925, the first in this collection of delicate, unique terra cotta Christmas figures handmade in Naples, Italy. This tradition continues today. It was the inspiration of St. Francis of Assisi in the 13th century, who created the first Nativity scenes using live people and animals to explain the birth of Jesus and the meaning and importance of the Nativity. Displaying crèche scenes became a beloved Christmas tradition in Italy in the 16th and 17th centuries. Naples is the central producer of these delicate figures

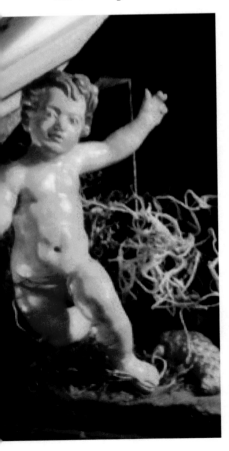

and angels, made of terra cotta and wood, dressed in artfully draped, opulent fabrics in luscious colors and minutely detailed accessories. In the 18th century, Don Carlos of Bourbon, the King of Naples, had about 6000 figures. Stage directors arranged the crèche displays in palaces and residences. Mrs. Howard included a Christmas tree with angels to her scene. The three wise men or magi, local citizens, scenic landscapes, village scenes, a variety of animals like goats, and even an elephant add to this remarkable tableau. Can you find the decorative lion? Naturally, the three wise men riding their camels are elegantly attired.

Years ago, I remember seeing Mrs. Howard on a forklift decorating her tree. What a delight it is to see her family following this annual custom. This beautiful tradition of creating Nativity scenes lives on, as a friend of mine is helping a family collect and display a crèche collection. Piped in Christmas music echoes throughout the medieval styled hall. Take time to look at all of the historic statues and sculptures too. The Met has many timely holiday concerts and tours. And check out the fantastic Met shops! Perfect for Christmas shopping, including their annual

unique Christmas tree ornament. Do go to the lower level at the entrance to the restaurant to see the miniature nummy sweet of the Met Museum decorated for the season. *(This is a sweetie!)*

From The Metropolitan Museum of Art you can take the cross-town bus at 84th Street just off Fifth Avenue, or walk along 86th Street with more shops like H&M and Barnes & Noble Bookstore, until you stand in front of the glistening tree at **Carl Schurz Park** on East End Avenue. On the first Sunday of December, there is a tree lighting with carol singing, entertainment and cocoa. Take the opportunity to walk around this park for dazzling views of the East River and Gracie Mansion. The entrance is at the end of 88th Street and East End Avenue. Can you believe that this 1799 farmhouse was out in the country when it was built? Now the official residence of the Mayor of the City of New York, tours are available. From the adjacent walkway, you can see illuminated boats and barges cruising up the East River. They toot their horns as I wave at them and sing "Jingle Bells." Adding to this festive and peaceful scene are the Christmas lights across the water in Queens and on the RFK Triborough and railroad bridges!

I always look forward to the Lilliputian store windows with creative Christmas scenes at "**Drug Mart,**" on the southwest corner of 86th Street and York Avenue. And look out, you may see Santa's Elf, dressed in her red coat, as this is my neighborhood.

El Museo Del Barrio at Fifth Avenue and East 105th sponsors The Three Kings Day Parade, a tradition in Spanish speaking countries on January 6th, when a processional winds through Harlem with live camels, music, floats and people wearing period costumes. This is great fun and a good way to explore this neighborhood and museum where the parade ends with a party.

As you know by now, I love to walk, explore and look up! During a recent Christmas at East 95th Street and First Avenue I was overwhelmed by a huge display of blow-up Santas, candy canes, luminaries, trees and even the Peanuts Family with a sign saying "Peace on Earth." I hope that this massive display comes back next year. I left a note and some candy canes!

Adjacent to El Museo Del Barrio is the renowned **Museum of the City of New York**, which specializes in all aspects of New York City History. Their videos on New York are worth seeing, as are their exhibitions, seasonal events and superb gift store. Located at 1220 Fifth Avenue the MCNY was founded in 1923.

Also on the Upper East Side is The **Society of Illustrators** at 128 East 63rd Street, located in a converted carriage house. It has the most incredible painting by Norman Rockwell called *Dover Coach*, showing merrymakers going home for Christmas. When Rockwell gave it to the Society in 1939, he explained that while painting it he was working in hot California and the riders of the coach were exasperated with the heat, which was augmented by their heavy clothes. *Dover Coach* hangs in the upstairs bar and excellent restaurant, where non-members can go for luncheon and other occasions. The balcony provides a good view of midtown Manhattan. The Society was founded in 1901 "to promote the art of illustration." There are interesting exhibits and collections all year and at Christmas they often have a show of children's illustrated books. It's another good, quiet, peaceful place to visit away from the holiday hustle and bustle!

For more historical revelry, go to the **Mount Vernon Hotel** at 421 East 61st Street to relive early 19th century Christmases with special holiday tours, lectures and music. The candlelight tours in this historic building are full of caroling, refreshments, and information about holiday customs and cooking in this period. This fieldstone building from 1799 is nestled amongst the skyscrapers of midtown. Originally a carriage house, it was where Abigail Adams Smith, daughter of John Adams, second president of the United States, lived. This charming structure became a hotel in 1826, when lower Manhattan was crowded and creeping uptown as a stopping place for travelers and for those who wanted to go to the country. We talk about pollution now, but can you imagine what life was like back then? The Colonial Dames of America have done a terrific job in developing this museum and its landscaped gardens.

WHITE CHRISTMAS

The best single selling record *(remember this is pre-digital times)* ever written is "White Christmas" by Irving Berlin, introduced in 1941 in the movie "Holiday Inn," and sung by Bing Crosby with Fred Astaire. Bing's recording became a huge hit right away and received the Academy Award in 1942. On Christmas Eve, it is a tradition to stand outside Berlin's former home at **17 Beekman Place,** east of 1st Avenue at 51st Street, and sing "White Christmas" and other carols. Kindly be considerate as Berlin's home is a private house. Check as often there are revivals of this Christmas classic. Sing along!! It is also interesting that until this time Christmas music was primarily sacred or carols. After the popularity of "White Christmas," more secular songs followed. In 1943 Bing also promoted "I'll Be Home for Christmas" (Gannon, Kent, Ram). In 1944 the beloved movie "Meet Me In St. Louis" introduced another favorite, "Have Yourself A Merry Little Christmas" (Hugh Martin and Ralph Blane), sung by Judy Garland. And remember "Rudolph the Red-nosed Reindeer," a song released in 1949, based on the popularity of a 1939 story by Montgomery Ward.

Music

The Pipes of Christmas is a Celtic tradition with bagpipes, brass, fiddles and special Celtic instruments. This festive event has taken place for seventeen years, with only two performances each season at **Madison Avenue Presbyterian Church** at East 73rd and Madison Avenue. Everyone does the Highland Fling after this spirited performance, which takes place on a weekend in early December.

Also in December, **Solomon R. Guggenheim Museum,** at 1071 Fifth Avenue at 88th Street presents a unique, melodious Christmas concert with the VOX chorus and orchestra moving around the swirling staircase and soaring interior. I was mesmerized watching the musicians move around the circular ramp!

* **The Metropolitan Museum of Art**
* **Church of the Heavenly Rest**
* **Church of Saint Ignatius Loyola**

Cuisine

At 2nd Avenue just south of 86th Street are the legendary German market and restaurant—**Schaller & Weber** and **The Heidelberg**. There was a large German population in this Upper

East Side area in the early 20th century with many breweries. The old Heidelberg is one of the last remaining German eateries in Yorkville. Their sauerkraut, sausages and sauerbraten are super! Many of these ingredients come from their neighbor,

Schaller & Weber, which has been selling German meats and sausages since the 1930s. At Christmas they have delicacies like pfeffernusse, a small spicy cookie, fruitcake and marzipan. You might see the Lady in Red buying my salami, cheese and other German delicacies!

Holiday Markets

Madison Avenue Christmas Street Fair stretching from 60th Street up to 72nd Street, opens in the beginning of December when Madison Avenue is closed off for a weekend with entertainment and refreshments. How special it is to be able to walk on the avenue with no traffic and look at the holiday windows. A portion of the money spent in the stores is donated to charities. Another worthwhile event!

IX
LOWER MANHATTAN

(STARTING FROM THE BOTTOM)

Stand at the head of **Wall Street** at Broadway and look down this narrow canyon lined with its impressive neoclassical buildings dedicated to finance. As times have changed, many are being adaptively reused as residences or commercial offices. I used to work on Wall Street and still chuckle that I once assumed it was wide and huge, but it turned out to be diminutive in scale. Walking around Lower Manhattan with medieval street plan is exhilarating and educational.

At the intersection of Wall Street and Broadway is historic **Trinity Church**, the third church on this site dating from 1846. The first Anglican Church opened here in 1697. This majestic Gothic Revival church has a 281-foot steeple and was the tallest building in Gotham until 1890. Be sure to go inside and hopefully you will hear the organ playing. Trinity is known for its superb music and has a professional choir, children's choir, Baroque Symphony and other musical groups.

Their annual Christmas musical programs include Handel's "Messiah," "The Twelve Days of Christmas," and the Christmas Eve and Day programs. When you sing "Silent Night" remember that in 1859 the Trinity minister, John Freeman Young, translated this German carol, launching its American debut. (*I hope that "all is calm" with you as you read this!*)

If you want a tranquil place, walk back to the chapel, which was added in 1913. I often go there to enjoy the peace and quiet. You are apt to see a lot of tourists in the Trinity Cemetery as Alexander Hamilton, more famous now due to the success of the musical "Hamilton," is buried here. Hamiltonites are flocking to the cemetery! It is fun to look at all the impressive gravestones and markers silhouetted against the skyscrapers of Wall Street.

Walk down Wall Street one block and on your left, at the head of Broad Street, George Washington is holding court at the **Federal Hall National Memorial,** the location where he was inaugurated as President in 1789. Someone has placed a wreath around our first President's head, perhaps remembering that the Washingtons once spent Christmas here.

On Broad Street you can see the **New York Stock Exchange** tree. Since 1923 the NYSE has had a superb tree in the middle of the street. At their tree lighting in early December, the season is hailed with wonderful music and sometimes the entertainment also includes The Rockettes! The facade of the NYSE building has brilliantly lit stars. Look up at the laughing lions on the pediment of this stately edifice. Are these beasties laughing at us—or the stock market? Where are the bulls and bears, the symbols of Wall Street? Don't look for bears! If you feel bullish walk back to Broadway and go south where the bull statue is a photo op.

Do go on a tour of the New York Stock Exchange and visit the Federal Hall Museum with many exhibits in its exquisite rotunda with Corinthian columns and a lofty belvedere, which provides a scenic view. Maybe you will be fortunate as I was and hear some caroling.

Continue down Wall Street for three blocks past many interesting structures. Be sure to look back up the street for another spectacular view of Trinity Church. Wall Street got its name because it was the northern boundary of the colonial settlement and a fence-like wall was put up to keep out animals and intruders.

Take a left on Water Street and walk up several blocks to Fulton Street and the **South Street Seaport**. The "Living Christmas Tree" is a 31-foot, steel frame filled with choristers silhouetted against a sparkling fifty-five feet tree and the masts of classic ships on the Hudson River. Christmas festivities start at Thanksgiving! The tree lighting takes place on "Giving Tuesday" after Thanksgiving. Lighted bands or "xylobands" are given out in advance, so go early to collect one. Choral groups like the Harlem Gospel Choir and Santa's Story perform on weekends. South Street Seaport, the former commercial and shipping hub of 19th century New York City, is now a Living Museum, still under reconstruction after super-storm Sandy did unbelievable damage!

Walk back up Fulton Street with its many eateries over to Broadway where you will see the oldest church in New York City, dating from 1766. The famed **St. Paul's Chapel,** part of Trinity Church, played such an important role in helping the wounded after 9/11 and was used by the firefighters as a sanctuary. The Church is now a memorial museum with touching displays. George Washington's pew when he lived here in 1789 is still there.

From St. Paul's Chapel you can see all the new skyscrapers that replaced and commemorate Ground Zero. A visit down here will be awesome and reflective. The winged, birdlike structure is the new architecturally unique transportation center by Santiago Calatrava, the famed Spanish architect, which just opened in 2016. The main hall inside, the **Oculus**, with enormous, intricate beams and glass panels, is filled with a variety of shops. The sunlight streaming in the windows is awesome and inspiring. Attached to The Oculus is the new **Eataly**, featuring a humongous array of Italian products and gourmet fare! (*Mangia bene!*)

Appreciate the setting of the **National September 11 Memorial & Museum.** The museum is touching and informative with photos, videos and objects. There is so much to learn and then take in the the tastefully designed plaza with the twin reflecting pools and the listing of the 2,983 people who valiantly died and will always be remembered. Count your blessings and then go across the street to Brookfield Place (West Street at 230 Vesey Street), the former World Financial Center site. The WFC was a dedicated Christmas supporter with the "Festival of Lights" in the Winter Garden, with 90-foot palm trees dressed for the season with 100,000 glistening lights. In 1997 Charles Dickens' great, great grandson talked about Dickens here and I heard him read from "A Christmas Carol." Brookfield Place is carrying on these Christmas traditions with many events, and all sorts of seasonal music in the stately palm court with blinking and vibrating lights. Brookfield has some holiday surprises on their plaza. This is a shopper and foodie paradise too! Step outside and watch the lights heralding the season on the boats on the Hudson River. Walk along the promenade to see the majestic **Statue of Liberty** and **Ellis Island**.

Walk back to Broadway and up to Canal Street, where there are a lot of Chinese restaurants and shops. Then walk up Mulberry Street to observe how Little Italy celebrates the spirit of Gothamtide. The oldest Italian community in the city has glittering, glitzy strings of lights and greenery strung across the street with other lively decorations. The aroma of food from the bustling restaurants and shops is enticing. The **Christmas In New York** store features all sorts of ornaments and gifts. The **Italian American Museum** at 155 Mulberry has many events and exhibits on the important Italian heritage. As Christmas is revered by Italians, there are many celebrations here and a gift shop too. Keep walking up Mulberry to East Houston Street, take a left and walk over several blocks to see the outdoor nativity scene at **Roman Catholic Church of Saint Anthony of Padua** at the corner of Sullivan Street. The figures are life size (*Or even bigger as I am so short!*). To my knowledge this is the only outdoor crèche scene in Manhattan.

Head north to **Washington Square Park**. In early December, Washington Square Park has the second oldest Christmas tree and carol lighting service, dating back to 1909. What a spectacular setting with the 45-feet tree adorned with multicolored lights silhouetted against the Washington Square arch. The

Christmas Eve festivities are memorable with Santa Claus leading the caroling and brass music too. *(Silent night!)*

Stroll around **Greenwich Village** to look at the historic
town houses dressed up for Gothamtide!

To appreciate how New Yorkers celebrated Christmas in
the 19th century a visit to the nearby **Merchant's House
Museum** at 29 East 4th Street, an 1832 Federal townhouse, is
a must! It is amazing that the Seabury Tredwell family lived here
with period furnishings and decor until the house became a museum in 1936 and later a National Landmark. The elegant Greek
Revival interiors with the fam-
ily's furnishings are traditionally decorated for the holidays
highlighting "Calling Day" or
"Cake Day." This Dutch New
Year's open-house tradition of
men visiting their friends to
wish them a happy New Year
was once the most important
holiday of the season. During
Colonial times, preparations for
New Year's Day started months
in advance, when the house was
cleaned and remodeled. There
was an impressive spread, including oysters and cookies (a
Dutch word). The favored drink
was punch and "punchmakers"
were booked in advance. Elegant
china and glassware were
used—even if they had to be
rented. "Artistes in hair" created elaborate coiffeurs for the
ladies of the household. It was

hoped that single daughters would meet potential male suitors. Men would visit their lists of friends and business contacts from early in the morning until late at night. In 1825, The Mayor of New York City, Philip Hone, noted in his diary that he made calls for five hours while his wife and daughters entertained one hundred and sixty-nine merrymakers. Men tried to make as many calls as possible to brag about. By the end of the 19th century the calling custom on New Year's Day had dwindled due to the rapid expansion of the city and the fanning out of friends into other neighborhoods. New York City is made up of many neighborhoods, which keep changing!

The Merchant's House Museum has many Christmas programs including the highly recommended reading of Charles Dickens' "A Christmas Carol," based on the author's readings on nearby 14th Street in 1867. I always go to hear the talented actor, John Kevin Jones, give his annual performance. The Bond Street Euterpean Singing Society has been musicians-in-residence for many years, performing "salon music" of the 19th century, classical and original music. It is magical to hear them perform in the elegant parlor. Euterpe is the muse of lyric poetry and music, and this group has many societies throughout the U.S. and Europe.

If you are interested in more Christmas music, walk up from Washington Square to 36–38 Fifth Avenue and West 10th Street to check out the **Church of the Ascension**, an Episcopal church completed in 1841 by Richard Upjohn who was also the architect of Trinity Church in Wall Street. In the next block, visit the **First Presbyterian Church** completed in 1846 by Joseph Wells.

X
UNION SQUARE, GRAMERCY PARK TO MADISON PARK

Continue up to 14th Street, turn right and walk over to Union Square. The Statue of George Washington will welcome you into the Christmas market. This wonderful European inspired tradition provides a festive experience with food, drink, entertainment and unique handcrafted gifts and artwork. The **Union Square Christmas Market** is revered for their "artisans pledge," which states that all merchandise is socially conscious and has inspired others in the city. Chat with the talented exhibitors, many from Vermont and western Pennsylvania, who welcome discussion of their crafts. Union Square was also the site of the first outdoor farmers market in 1976, which started a movement and today there are over thirty similar markets in New York City.

There are many ways to go from here. Stroll up Broadway to the socially conscious **ABC Carpets** on Broadway and East 17th Street, with inspiring Christmas windows that reflect their "fair and square" corporate philosophy, which includes good designs that are often handmade, community-produced and recyclable. I remember the Gandhi quote, "be the change that you want to see in the world" that was featured one year. Inside you can learn about the many visionary organizations that the ABC Home & Planet Foundation supports for global and local change. There are so many interesting presents and also a wonderful restaurant. *(Num!)* For over twenty-five years this store has had special weekend Santa events with stories and songs from the North Pole. I often see the same families returning each year and I love their theme "Christmas isn't Christmas until Santa arrives."

Stroll over to **Gramercy Park** at East 20th to 21st Streets, a gated park with a spectacularly decorated Christmas tree, a gift from a family for over forty years. This park is private and residents have keys. However, on Christmas Eve you can enter the park for an hour for caroling. *(What a special place to fa-la-la and ho-ho-ho!)*

Walking towards Gramercy Park South I always look at the magnificent tree at the **National Arts Club**, which was originally built as a private home in 1884. This handsome Gothic Revival house was converted into a club specializing in the arts and has some Christmas events open to the public. *Ho-ho-ho!* Now head over to Madison Square Park for more merriment.

Madison Square Park at Fifth Avenue between East 23rd to 26th Streets is the site of the first public Christmas tree in 1912. My hero, the social reformer Jacob Riis, realized that there were a lot of people who could not afford to have a

tree, so he helped to obtain a 70-feet tree from the Adirondacks, had it erected in Madison Square, adorned with Edison's lights. He arranged a carol singing evening. A "Star of Hope" monument marks this historic spot. Every year Madison Square has a notable tree with special ornaments, A Taste of Home Gingerbread Boulevard (with nummy recipes), caroling and lots of other festivities.

Cuisine

The Flatiron area is so "in," with **Eataly NYC Flatiron**, a vibrant Italian marketplace at 200 Fifth Avenue. It features an array of cafes, counters, restaurants and, across the street, a cooking school. Be sure to take in this lively, expanding neighborhood! The Flatiron building at the intersection of Fifth Avenue, Broadway and 23rd Street is iconic because of its "iron" like shape.

Near Gramercy Park on Irving Place is the fabled **Pete's Tavern** at 129 East 18th Street, the oldest bar and restaurant in Gotham dating from 1864. The awning welcomes you with "The Tavern that O. Henry made famous." O. Henry wrote "The Gift of the Magi" from 1904 to 1906. He lived nearby and you can actually sit in O' Henry's booth, gaze at his photo and be inspired. The ceiling lights add to the lively Christmas scene. The cuisine is Italian-American.

Other nearby eateries include **Rolf's** at 281 3rd Avenue and East 21st Street, known for its elaborate holiday decorations. Enjoy garlands of greenery, glitzy vintage ornaments, twinkling lights —and hearty German fare! This is a spectacular display, but if too crowded take a look and then go up one block to **Molly's** at 287 3rd Avenue, which also has splendid lights, but is quieter.

XI
UPTOWN—WEST SIDE

*F*or many years at the beginning of December the streets of the West Side (from 59th Street to 66th Street) are filled with food booths and Christmas festivities for one night. The "Winter's Eve at Lincoln Center" tree lighting at **Lincoln Center for the Performing Arts** heralds the season with the illumination of their unique tree decorated with musical instrument ornaments. Down the street the multi-storied **Time Warner Center** has many shops and eateries in their lobby. At Columbus Circle is the brilliantly lit "Holiday Under the Stars" with twelve 14-feet long stars, which change colors and play Christmas music and everyone sings. I just love this spectacular star show! Scurry up the escalator and you can watch this incredible sight and look out at the amazing view of Christopher Columbus atop his column in Columbus Circle at the entrance of Central Park. Visit **The Holiday Market at Columbus Circle**. And of course there are many Christmas entertainments at Lincoln Center, together with its affiliate the **Rose Jazz Center** in the Time Warner Building. If you are a jazz fan, this is a must.

There are also many other holiday concerts at Lincoln Center, including **The Metropolitan Opera, the New York Philharmonic at David Geffen Hall** and **Alice Tully Hall**, with many "Messiahs," the New Year's "Salute to Vienna" and the Big Apple Circus.

The Nutcracker at **David A. Koch Theater** is a Gothamtide tradition. Did you know that The Nutcracker was a story created in Germany in 1816 by E.T.A. Hoffmann? There were several versions but in 1892 the ballet opened in St. Petersburg, Russia, with music by Tchaikovsky. In 1944 the first presentation in America took place in San Francisco. The most popular version by George Balanchine opened in New York in 1954. (*Thanks to New York City again!*)

Tavern on the Green in Central Park at West 70th Street and Central Park West was built as a sheep stable in 1870. Converted to an eatery in 1934, their Christmas displays with 260,000 little white lights and illuminated topiaries of a bear and unicorn are legendary. Times have changed! With lots of Christmas decorations, the restaurant is still festive! This setting has an excellent vantage point for looking at the shining and shimmering Manhattan skyline dressed for the season.

Stroll up to the "mammoth" **American Museum of Natural History** on Central Park West between West 79th to 81st Streets where the Macy's Thanksgiving Day parade revelry begins! Entering the museum on Central Park West, you will be greeted by holiday lighted dinosaurs made of greenery. Look for the sculpted deer in the concrete bench and rest if you are tired. It always gives me joy knowing that Teddy Roosevelt, President of the United States and one of the founders of this museum, was an activist for animals, the environment, social reform and a buddy of my hero the social reformer and photographer, Jacob Riis. When you enter the AMNH a spectacular fifteen-feet tree adorned with thousands of intricately folded paper origami ornaments will overwhelm you! Each year a different symbolic theme, like dinosaurs or fish, is selected for the volunteers crafting these delicate delights based on the Japanese custom, and demonstrations are given. *(Good grief—I wouldn't have the patience!)* But it is such a delight learning about other holiday traditions.

This museum has so many treasures including dinosaurs, minerals, gems, and other stuffed animals. Have fun exploring! Their superb planetarium features "Starry Nights"—a perfect thing to see at Christmas! **Kwanzaa** is celebrated at The Museum of Natural History on December 31.

Across the street is the **New-York Historical Society** at West 77th Street, which contains so much Christmas history. This venerable institution was founded in 1804 by Knickerbockers, including Washington Irving and John Pintard, as a way to promote New York and St. Nicholas. The N-YHS has the original "Santa Claus—Good Holy Man" broadside—poem that I referred to before as being important in the spread of Santa Claus and Christmas. The N-YHS has original books by Washington Irving, one of four copies of Clement Clarke Moore's "A Visit from St.Nicholas," and many doc-

uments and treasures about Christmas. Also in the collection are medals and papers from the St. Nicholas Society, which was founded in 1835 to support New York's Dutch Heritage and has annual dinners. The N-YHS has festive exhibitions, lectures, and a gift store featuring Christmas. Do fit this into your holiday plans! Ask to see Clement Clarke Moore's desk, which is part of the N-YHS collection. Maybe this will inspire you to write a Gothamtide ditty?

XII
FURTHER UPTOWN—
WEST SIDE

*F*urther uptown is the magnificent Gothic Revival **Church of the Intercession** on 155th and Broadway, built between 1910 and 1914 and designed by one of my favorite architects, Bertram Goodhue who is buried here.

The church hosts a First Sunday in December with a **Clement Clarke Moore Candlelight Carol Service**. This inspiring service dates back to 1910 and often features a renowned person who reads "A Visit" at the church. Held in the late afternoon, the service is accompanied by spirited music, often the Harlem Boys Choir. Afterwards, Old St. Nicholas gives out lighted lanterns and leads everyone across the street to the historic Trinity Cemetery, where Clement Clarke Moore, who supposedly wrote "A Visit from St. Nicholas," is buried. After winding down this long incline, carols are sung at his tombstone followed by hot cocoa. *(Oh joy!)* This is one of my favorite events; it is so special hearing "A Visit" in this glorious interior and then walking through the cemetery with a view of the majestic Hudson River. Be prepared in case of snow or rain!

The Cathedral of St. John the Divine (1047 Amsterdam Avenue at West 112th Street), was begun in 1892 and is still not finished. This soaring and spectacular Gothic Revival cathedral, the largest

in the U.S., has many seasonal activities: in addition to a Christmas market, the acclaimed Paul Winter's Annual Winter Solstice performance with music, dancing and gospel singing. Also featured are "revels" with bagpipes, jugglers, and Morris dancers, the performance of Handel's "Messiah" and a New Year's Eve service. If you are free on Christmas Day there are always Christmas concerts with musical traditions from different countries. Explore the whole complex at St. John the Divine and then wander a few blocks up to see the architecturally rich Columbia University.

Located even further uptown, **The Cloisters** are in picturesque **Fort Tryon Park** overlooking the Hudson River at approximately 192nd Street. To escape the festive frenzy it is a joy to go to this quiet branch of The Metropolitan Museum, which incorporates parts of five European ecclesiastical cloisters, chapels, and architectural components dating from the 12th to 15th centuries. The Cloisters are filled with medieval treasures, including stained glass, sculptures, paintings and the famous intricately woven and symbolic "Unicorn" tapestries. Just being at the Cloisters is soothing and peaceful with recorded medieval music. There are highly regarded concerts and lectures year-round. The Christmas themed ones, when the Cloisters is decorated with period medieval-styled greens and preserved grasses is the best. (Book in advance!).

Look up at a chandelier enveloped in a huge "furry hay"

wreath tied with a red bow. This intricately woven wreath made out of Kansas wheat was inspired by similar ones in medieval German churches, a guide told me. Gothamtide provides so many opportunities to learn about different holiday customs from around the world.

Be sure to go outside to enjoy the renowned garden with over 250 species of plants and find the adjacent **Trie Cloister**. The first capital on a column in the south arcade depicts the Nativity on one side and a bagpiper and lamb on the other. How I enjoy looking for beasties and other ornaments that depict the imagery of Gothamtide!

And enjoy the incredible landscape with dramatic views of the Big Apple, Hudson River, and George Washington Bridge, and across the river New Jersey, the Garden State. Look down. Do you see a red lighthouse? This is the storied **"The Little Red Lighthouse and the Great Gray Bridge,"** a book published in 1951 by Hildegarde Hoyt Swift. This lighthouse was erected in 1921 because of the perilous shoals in the turbulent river. After O. H. Ammann and Cass Gilbert completed the modernistic George Washington Bridge in

1931 with many lights, the lighthouse was supposed to be auctioned off or torn down, but this charming icon was so greatly admired that it was saved and is now open to the public. Do visit!

XIII
GOTHAMTIDE
HIGHLIGHTS

Trees & Lights

As noted before, public Christmas trees really got started in 1912 when Jacob Riis helped to bring a tree from upstate New York to Madison Square so everyone could enjoy its majesty. I like the recent use of LED lighting and there are more and more lit trees everywhere both inside and outside. Some stay illuminated all year long and in my neighborhood, I walk past a building every day with several balconies adorned with different color lights.

Here are some of my favorite outside trees:
* **Rockefeller Center** (*see Rockefeller Center*)
* **Park Avenue** (*see Park Avenue Lights to Grand Central*)
* **Carl Schurz Park** (*see Upper East Side*)
* **Washington Square Park** (*see Lower Manhattan from Wall Street to 14th Street*)
* **Lincoln Center** (*see Upper West Side from Columbus Avenue*)
* **Lotte New York Palace Hotel** (*see Fifth Avenue —Gothamtide Tour*)

Carols, Music & Churches

Christmas carols grew out of the sacred music traditions of Franciscan and Dominican orders, as well as the earlier rounds sung at the Winter Solstice celebrations when people danced around stone circles. Some of the carols that we sing today are 19th century American: "It Came Upon a Midnight Clear" written by Edmund Sears in 1849, a Unitarian Minister in Massachusetts; "Jingle Bells" written by James Lord Pierpont of Boston in 1856. In New York at the General Theological Seminary, Rev. John H. Hopkins wrote the lyrics and composed "We Three Kings of Orient Are," for a Christmas pageant in 1857. Do visit General Theological Seminary in Chelsea for more music.

I recently discovered that "The Santa Claus Symphony," written by William Henry Fry of Philadelphia in 1853, is available as a CD and is a delightful romp all year long! *(Fa-la-la!)*

I just love all the music during the holiday season everywhere in Gotham. So often merrymakers just join together and sing spontaneously. I have witnessed this at Rockefeller Center. I feel "My Tree" inspires one to sing.

There are so many versions of the "Messiah" and the Nutcracker all over the city and other holiday "carol" concerts —both classical and modern. And you can even hear music from holiday displays on the facades of Cartier's at 52nd Street.

Here are some of my other favorite holiday musical events:

- ❄ **Carnegie Hall** *(see 5th Avenue Gothamtide Lane Tour)*
- ❄ **Saint Thomas Church** *(see 5th Avenue Gothamtide Lane Tour)*
- ❄ **Saint Patrick's Cathedral** *(see 5th Avenue Gothamtide Lane Tour)*
- ❄ **21 Club**—singing with the Salvation Army *(see 5th Avenue Gothamtide Lane)*

* **Saint Bartholomew's** *(see Park Avenue Lights to Grand Central)*
* **Solomon R. Guggenheim Museum** *(see Upper East Side)*
* **Church of the Heavenly Rest** *(see Upper East Side)*
* **Saint Ignatius Loyola** *(see Upper East Side)*
* **Irving Berlin Christmas Eve sing-along** *(see Upper East Side)*
* **Church of Saint Mary the Virgin** *(see Park Avenue Lights to Grand Central)*
* **Madison Avenue Presbyterian Church** *(see Upper East Side)*
* **Trinity Church** *(see Lower Manhattan from Wall Street to 14th Street)*
* **Cathedral of Saint John the Divine** *(see Upper West Side from Columbus Avenue)*
* **Church of the Ascension** *(see Lower Manhattan from Wall Street to 14th Street)*
* **First Presbyterian Church** *(see Lower Manhattan from Wall Street to 14th Street)*

Stores, Boutiques, Christmas Markets & Shopping

As New York City prospered the first department store, A.T. Stewart's, opened in 1848 on Lower Broadway at Chambers Street. Many other department stores followed. The building still stands and has been through many chapters. By 1867 holiday gift buyers were "storming the stores."

Today the unveiling of the big department store windows is always gleefully anticipated at Gothamtide. The work that goes on behind these spectacular vignettes is awesome. The growth of technology and LED lighting has produced amazing lighting, displays and music. A designer of Saks Christmas finery told me that they start planning right after New Year's! *(Ask questions. You can learn a lot too!)*

The grand opening of the store windows and other Christmas displays is amazing. The entertainment can include fireworks, sacred and popular singing groups, The Rockettes and lots of Christmas characters, including camels, sheep, Santa Clauses, Mrs. Santa Claus, elves, and Mickey Mouse—you name it! In recent years the sound and light shows have been exhilarating! I was so excited when I met

Santa Claus at Lord & Taylor. We had our photo taken while listening to the caroling by one of my favorite singing groups, Young People's Chorus of New York City. Walk west on 34th Street one block to Broadway and you will be rewarded with Macy's.

Since Broadway is now closed to vehicles, take advantage of the pedestrian plaza with tables and chairs. Get refreshment from one of the vendors on Herald Square, relax and take in the merrymakers. Since the 1940s, the animated clock (1895) that was originally on top of the *New York Herald* newspaper building across the street (demolished) has been the icon of this little plaza. Look up at Minerva, the goddess of wisdom, instructing the bell ringers to keep the time. Look for the owls too.

Store windows

❊ **Macy's** (*see 5th Avenue Gothamtide Lane Tour*)
❊ **Lord & Taylor** (*see 5th Avenue Gothamtide Lane Tour*)
❊ **Bergdorf Goodman** (*see 5th Avenue Gothamtide Lane Tour*)
❊ **Barneys** (*see 5th Avenue Gothamtide Lane Tour*)
❊ **Dolce & Gabbana** (*see 5th Avenue Gothamtide Lane Tour*)
❊ **Harry Winston** (*see 5th Avenue Gothamtide Lane Tour*)
❊ **Anthropologie** (*see Rockefeller Center*)
❊ **Tiffany & Co.** (*see 5th Avenue Gothamtide Lane Tour*)
❊ **ABC Carpets** (*see Union Square, Gramercy Park to Madison Park*)

Holiday Outdoor Markets

This wonderful tradition based on the European Christmas markets provides a festive experience with food, drink, entertainment and a wonderful opportunity to buy unique, handcrafted, organic, creative gifts and artwork.

* **Union Square** (*see Union Square, Gramercy Park to Madison Park*)
* **Little Italy** (*see Lower Manhattan*)
* **Madison Avenue Christmas Street Fair** (*see Upper East Side*)
* **Columbus Circle Holiday Market** (*see Upper West Side from Columbus Avenue*)
* **Bryant Park** (*see 5th Avenue Gothamtide Lane Tour*)
* **Grand Central Terminal** —the only holiday market that is inside! (*see Park Avenue Lights to Grand Central*)

Cuisine

Around the world, feasting and food have always been a major part of holiday festivities! Wouldn't you know that Charles Dickens and his friend Washington Irving promoted the great feast, family gatherings, and entertainment in their writings and talks! For many the celebrations went on for twelve days. Essayist James Henry Leigh Hunt expressed this in 1840: "Christmas day was the morning of the season; New Year's Day the middle of it or noon; Twelfth Night is the night, brilliant with Twelfth Night cakes"

Good ol' Dickens popularized turkey, which had been introduced to England in 1523 to 1543 from America. Don't you remember that in *A Christmas Carol* Scrooge after his revelations on Christmas morning says to a young lad passing by, "...not the little turkey, the big one" for the Cratchit family!" Be sure to savor the New York City tradition and aroma of chestnuts roasting in the streets from multiple food vendors.

Please note I'm only mentioning eateries where I have happily dined.

* **Brasserie Ruhlmann** *(see Rockefeller Center)*
* **Sea Grill** *(see Rockefeller Center)*
* **Rock Center Cafe** *(see Rockefeller Center)*
* **21 Club** *(see Rockefeller Center)*
* **Rolf's** *(see Union Square, Gramercy Park to Madison Avenue)*
* **Molly's** *(see Union Square, Gramercy Park to Madison Avenue)*
* **Pete's Tavern** *(see Union Square, Gramercy Park to Madison Avenue)*
* **Old Heidelberg** *(see Upper East Side)*
* **Schaller & Weber** *(see Upper East Side)*
* **Tavern on the Green** *(see Upper West Side from Columbus Avenue in Central Park at West 70th Street and Central Park West)*

Creative Teams

Accolades to the creators of the glittering and glowing Gothamtide windows and displays. There are many creative teams but these I know best!

Lou Nasti—Mechanical Displays of Brooklyn is the magical world of animated holiday and Christmas displays. Lou started creating his inventive displays in 1969 and is now busier than ever. Among his award-winning inspirations are the red bow around Cartier's on Fifth Avenue and the many moving and singing creations for the Fisher Brothers office buildings! My favorite has been the "Bears Christmas," with about ninety bears and fourteen penguins making gifts, skating, having coffee at Starbears, caroling and dancing with Leonard Bearstein and enjoying Christmas. This all-time favorite was at Park Avenue Plaza behind the Racquet Club on Park Avenue between 52nd and 53th Streets. As it was so magical, my Gothamtide tours started here, Lou often talked to my merrymakers and he invited me to watch his "magicians" assemble these intricate displays! (My website and Facebook photos are in front of the bears.)

The lobby was modernized recently and my favorite display is gone! Nasti's magic can be seen in Indiana, Texas, Arkansas, Baltimore and even Australia. Many years ago, he created holiday windows for Higbee's Department Store in Cleveland, Ohio. When Higbee's was converted to a casino, Lou was asked to recreate these windows, which everyone loves! (mechanicaldisplays.com 718-258-5588 - Brooklyn, NY)

American Christmas—Fred Schwam—This is the second generation of Schwams who have created so many holiday displays. I love their motto—"Passionately decorating the halls since 1968." A few of their notable installations include many of the buildings at Rockefeller Center, the Candy Canes on the Avon Building on West 57th Street and the magnificent lighting on the Harry Winston store on Fifth Avenue and 56th Street. Their "Palace" lighting and music on the facade of Saks Fifth Avenue is so popular with crowds of admirers. (www.americanxmas.com - 914-663-0600 - Mount Vernon, NY)

For Collectors of Christmas Decorations & Memorabilia

The Golden Glow of Christmas Past is a special organization for collectors of Christmas ornaments, decorations and lighting — vintage to more recent times. With over 1200 members, there is a magazine that comes out six times a year with interesting articles about various collectibles. Their Annual Meetings in various locations are so festive with lectures, tours, dealers and merriment.

An annual membership costs $50 — for more information contact goldenglow.org. When you join, you get a directory of the members, who are willing to share their knowledge. (A "glowing" group!)

National Christmas Center—Founded by the dedicated "Santa" Jim Morrison, who has collected the most incredible Christmas memorabilia with fifteen different galleries, including: "Santa's North Pole and Reindeer Barn; a 1950s Woolworth 5&10 store; Christmas Around the World; the Toyland Train Mountain. If you are a Christmas fancier, do plan a visit. Many people come from all over the world to see this unique and joyful Christmas center. 3427 Lincoln Highway (Route 30), Paradise, Lancaster County, PA www.NationalChristmasCenter.com Phone 717-442-7950.

"So the shortest day came,
and the year died...
Came people singing, dancing,
To drive the dark away...
As promise awakens in the sleeping land:
They carol, feast, give thanks,
And dearly love their friends,
and hope for peace.
And so do we, here, now,
This and every year.
Welcome Yule!"

—from "Revels," an English Christmas
tradition at the Emma Willard School

Acknowledgements

Through the years of my Gothamtide research, writing, lecturing and tours, the following are my Christmas elves, who taught, showed, listened, advised and encouraged Queen Santa. Continue to "sprinkle joy."

Laura Anghelone, Kristy Askey, Kathleen Bennett, Robert Burden, William Canup, Jennifer Carlquist, Julia Garrett Clay, Justin Ferate, Ann Garrett, Sarah Hock, Janice Langrall, Peyton Grubbs Lister, CJ Love, Mary Anne Hunting, Pauline Metcalf, "Santa" Jim Morrison, Victoria Neel, Jean Marie Nobile, James Russiello, Sarah Garrett Simms, Jeanne Solensky, Richard E. Slavin III, Wilson Stiles; Staff of Brasserie Ruhlmann, 21 Club, NBCStore and Tours, New-York Historical Society, New York Public Library, NYCVP, the Rockefeller Center Staff, Winterthur Museum and Library.

**"I have always thought of Christmas as a good time;
A kind, forgiving, generous, pleasant time;
A time when men and women seem to open hearts freely
And so I say "God Bless Christ-
mas."**

—Charles Dickens

Photo Credits

iii, v, vi, 2, 19, 71, 99, 102, 125; original silk-screen art by John A. Martine , circa 1955, used with permission

ii, viii, 4, 52, 58, 62, 64, 108, 118; photographs by Brooke Slezak©, 2016, used with permission

6, 15, 31, 34, 39, 43, 44, 48, 72, 73, 77, 104, 107, 116, 121, 122, 124; 128, from the author's collection

24; Macy's, photograph by Katie Larsen-Lick©, 2015, used with permission

26, 27, 72 (top); photographs by James Russiello©, 2013, used with permission

33; *Prometheus by Paul Manship at Rockefeller Center,* photograph by Kowloonese/WikiCommons, 2004

40 (top and bottom), 50, 51; Brasserie Ruhlmann©, photographs, 2016, used with permission

47; *Song,* Radio City Music Hall, mixed metal and enamel by Hildreth Meière, 1932, Photograph by Hildreth Meière Dunn; 2015, used with permission

59; Dolce & Gabanna angel, photograph by Kathleen Bennett, 2014, used with permission

61; Saint Thomas Church, used with permission

63; 21 Club, artist unknown, used with permission

69; NYPL Lions Patience and Fortitude, public domain

76; Narthex looking north, St. Bartholomew's Church, with domes in glass mosaic by Hildreth Meière, 1930; photograph by Hildreth Meière Dunn, 2015, used with permission.

77; Park Avenue lights, illustration by Victoria Neel, used with permission

78; New York Transit Museum entrance, poster by Marcin Wichary/WikiCommons, 2007

80; The Young People's Chorus of New York City performs at the Metropolitan Museum of Art for the annual tree lighting ceremony, photograph by Christpher Hall/WikiCommons, 2012

82; Neapolitan cherub, photograph by Jonathan Preece©, 2016

83; Neopolitan angel, photograph, The Metropolitan Museum of Art, used with permission

85; *Dover Coach*, painting by Norman Rockwell/Society of Illustrators, 1938, used with permission

86; White Christmas movie poster, 1954, public domain

90; The NYSE at Christmas time, photograph by Massimo Catarinella/Wikipedia, 2008

92; Trinity Church from a suspended scaffold, photograph by William Canup, 2016, used with permission

96; The Arch and Yule tree at Washington Square Park, New York, photograph by Ciar/WikiCommons, 2007

97, 98; Merchant's House, interior and exterior; used with permission

108; Church of the Intercession Clement Clarke Moore Candlelight Carol Service, *The New York Times*, photograph by Leah Reddy, 2014

100; Christmas Tree in the Christmas Market at Union Square, New York, photograph by Deror Avi/WikiCommons, 2007

111; Red Stag with Golden Antlers (detail of stained glass panel at the Cloisters–done around 1350), source: federfiles.com

128; First Christmas card, designed by John Callcott Horsley for Henry Cole, 1843

To a giving, glorious,
glittering, glimmering and
gleeful Gothamtide!
Hohoho!!

QUEEN SANTA, THE ELF
& LADY IN RED

Made in the USA
Lexington, KY
16 November 2018